PRAISE FOR *Forty Ways to Look at Winston Churchill*

"A compelling read . . . that achieves the considerable feat of distilling an epic life to its essence while deconstructing the art of biography. *Forty Ways to Look at Winston Churchill* does for the writing of history what Wallace Stevens's 'Thirteen Ways of Looking at a Blackbird' did for poetry—both does it and shows us how it's done."

—JAMES ATLAS, author of *Bellow: A Biography*

"Was there ever a better subject for biography? Heroic, petty, noble, selfish, courageous, devious, grandiloquent, plain-speaking, generous, tyrannical, Churchill was all these and more. Rubin strives to capture the essence of her larger-than-life subject not through a head-on assault, but by circling him and taking snapshots from a multiplicity of angles. Her *Forty Ways to Look at Winston Churchill* is a feat of intelligent compression, a stereoscopic portrait for the space age, a biography in miniature, and not least, a rattling good read."

—MICHAEL SCAMMELL, author of *Solzhenitsyn: A Biography*

"An excellent introduction to one of the most written-about men in history . . . Rubin's unique approach works surprisingly well, bringing fresh insight to an exhaustively covered subject."

—*Publishers Weekly*

PHOTO: © DAVE CROSS

GRETCHEN RUBIN received her undergraduate and law degrees from Yale and was editor-in-chief of the *Yale Law Journal*. She clerked for Justice Sandra Day O'Connor of the U.S. Supreme Court and served as counsel to Federal Communications Commission Chairman Reed Hundt. She teaches at Yale Law School and School of Management and is the author of *Power Money Fame Sex: A User's Guide*.

Visit the author's website at www.gretchenrubin.com.

Forty Ways to Look at
WINSTON CHURCHILL

By Gretchen Rubin

Forty Ways to Look at Winston Churchill

Power Money Fame Sex: A User's Guide

Forty Ways
to Look at
WINSTON
CHURCHILL

A Brief Account of a Long Life

Gretchen Rubin

RANDOM HOUSE TRADE PAPERBACKS
NEW YORK

2004 Random House Trade Paperback Edition

This work was originally published in hardcover by Ballantine Books, an imprint of The Random House Publishing Group, a division of Random House, Inc., New York, in 2003.

Library of Congress Cataloging-in-Publication Data

Rubin, Gretchen Craft.
   Forty ways to look at Winston Churchill : a brief account of a long life / Gretchen Rubin.
     p. cm.
   Originally published: New York : Ballantine Books, 2003.
   Includes bibliographical references and index.
   ISBN 0-8129-7144-2 (trade) — ISBN 1-58836-384-8 (G-book)
    1. Churchill, Winston, Sir, 1874–1965.   2. Prime ministers—Great Britain—Biography.   3. Great Britain—Politics and government—20th century.   I. Title: 40 ways to look at Winston Churchill.   II. Title.

DA566.9.C5R79 2004
941.084'092—dc22
[B]   2003069318

www.atrandom.com

Text design by C. Linda Dingler

Manufactured in the United States of America

10 9 8 7 6 5 4 3 2

To my mother and father

We shall go on to the end. We shall fight in France, we shall fight on the seas and oceans, we shall fight with growing confidence and growing strength in the air, we shall defend our Island, whatever the cost may be. We shall fight on the beaches, we shall fight on the landing grounds, we shall fight in the fields and in the streets, we shall fight in the hills; we shall never surrender.

—WINSTON CHURCHILL, ADDRESS TO THE HOUSE OF COMMONS
JUNE 4, 1940

Many scenes have come & gone unwritten, since it is today the 4th Sept, a cold grey blowy day, made memorable by the sight of a kingfisher, & by my sense, waking early, of being again visited by "the spirit of delight." "Rarely rarely comest thou, spirit of delight." That was I singing this time last year; & sang so poignantly that I have never forgotten it, or my vision of a fin rising on a wide blank sea. No biographer could possibly guess this important fact about my life in the late summer of 1926: yet biographers pretend they know people.

—VIRGINIA WOOLF, *Diaries*
SEPTEMBER 4, 1927

CONTENTS

Forty Ways to Look at
WINSTON CHURCHILL

INTRODUCTION

I know exactly when my obsession with Winston Churchill began: on a plane from New York City to Anchorage, while I was reading a World War II history that described a scene at Churchill's country house. Prime Minister Churchill, we learn, had standing orders that he was to be awakened before 8:00 A.M. only if Britain itself was invaded. Sometime after 8:00 one morning in 1941, Foreign Secretary Anthony Eden answered a knock by Churchill's valet, who presented him with a cigar on a silver tray. "The Prime Minister's compliments, and the German armies have invaded Russia." Churchill—what a character! Not to be disturbed in sleep even for such extraordinarily good news for Britain. And then to celebrate by sending around a cigar, with that wonderful message, "The Prime Minister's compliments, and the German armies have invaded Russia."

I wanted to read more. Like many people born after Churchill's death in 1965, I knew little about him. He'd been a great Prime Minister during that war, and he'd given a famous speech about "this was their finest hour," and after

Lady Astor snapped, "Winston, if I were your wife, I'd put poison in your coffee," he'd retorted, "Nancy, if I were your husband, I'd drink it." That was about the extent of my knowledge. I dog-eared the page to remind myself to track down a Churchill biography.

But later at the library, the huge and often multivolume biographies daunted me, and when I turned instead to read Churchill himself, I faced his five-volume history of World War I, his six-volume history of World War II, and his four-volume history of the English-speaking peoples. I didn't know where to start. I wanted to know *something* about Churchill but not *everything* about him.

But I was lucky. I made just the right choice—Churchill's partial memoir, *My Early Life*. The man was a James Bond who'd *actually lived,* the hero of a novel that really happened. I was enthralled by Churchill's fantastic successes and failures, by his outsize character, and by his historic vision. And his writing was so masterful—I found myself rereading passages to savor his words. "The senior officers consulted together. As so often happens when things go wrong formalities were discarded, and I found myself taking part in the discussion." Of his obnoxious ambition as a young soldier, Churchill wrote:

> The expressions "Medal-hunter" and "Self-advertiser" were used from time to time . . . in a manner which would, I am sure, surprise and pain the readers of these notes. It is melancholy to be forced to record these less amiable aspects of human nature, which by a most curious and indeed unaccountable coincidence have always

seemed to present themselves in the wake of my innocent footsteps.

The book's closing paragraph was unforgettable: "Events were soon to arise in the fiscal sphere which were to plunge me into new struggles and absorb my thoughts and energies at least until September 1908, when I married and lived happily ever afterwards." He published this memoir in 1930.

After that first book, I read one volume after another about Churchill and by Churchill. The scope of his life and experience overwhelmed me: just consider that Churchill was born in 1874 (the American Civil War ended in 1865) and lived to age ninety, entered Parliament first in 1900 at age twenty-five, held seven Cabinet positions between 1908 and 1940, was Prime Minister twice, and finally retired in 1964, at age eighty-nine. He lived in a time of tremendous change: he fought in a British cavalry charge using lances as weapons; already a Cabinet member in 1910, Churchill urged that Britain contact the *Wright brothers*—he'd heard about the invention of the *airplane*; he died the year Malcolm X was shot.

As I plunged into his life, a truth (often noted, often overlooked) confronted me: Churchill's portrait could be drawn in innumerable ways, all "true." I was struck to see his biographers reach different conclusions from the same facts. Was Churchill a military genius or a meddling amateur? Was he a great defender of liberty or a reactionary imperialist? Was he a success or a failure? Once I had command of the material, I amused myself by tracing how each account exaggerated certain details, and slid over others, to support its conclusions.

Some issues are complex, so it's unsurprising that biographers weigh the evidence differently or reach contradictory conclusions. But often even a seemingly straightforward fact takes on a different character when related by different biographers. For example, in his fascinating account *The Duel: Hitler vs. Churchill,* John Lukacs observes, "Churchill, unlike Hitler, was a man of unrepressed feelings. Tears, on some occasions, would come into his eyes." This is *quite* an understatement. Churchill in fact cried often and abundantly—"he could have filled buckets" according to one colleague. Perhaps Lukacs didn't feel comfortable with the notion of a weepy Churchill.

Sometimes I'd detect a biographer's reading too much into facts—supplying motives or states of mind—without any apparent evidence. William Manchester's engaging biography *Churchill: Visions of Glory* describes a photograph of Churchill's mother, Jennie Jerome, when she was in her late teens: "Dark, vivacious, and magnificent, she stands alone, staring boldly at the photographer, her left arm outflung, the hand atop a furled umbrella, her hips cocked saucily. It is almost a wanton pose, the posture of a virgin who can hardly wait to assume another position." How in the world, I asked myself as I studied the picture, did Manchester come up with all *that*? To me, it looked like a picture of a mother and her three daughters, decked out in Victorian finery. True, Jennie had her hand on an umbrella, and true, later in her life she'd have many lovers, but her hips didn't look cocked, and her posture certainly didn't look *wanton*. This description seemed to tell more about Manchester than about Jennie Jerome.

The distortions of a writer's viewpoint are even more apparent in a memoir. The "diary" of Churchill's carping, self-important doctor Lord Moran is an amusing example of dramatic irony: there's quite a gap between what Lord Moran said happened and what the reader thinks happened. Lord Moran relates a conversation with Churchill about Churchill's fits of depression, or "black dog," which Moran considered quite serious. Moran said:

> "Your trouble—I mean the Black Dog business—you got from your forebears. You have fought against it all your life. That is why you dislike visiting hospitals. You always avoid anything that is depressing."
>
> Winston stared at me as if I knew too much.

Conceited Lord Moran *thought* Churchill stared at him as if he knew too much. I suspected Churchill was thinking "Cheek!" or "No, I don't like visiting hospitals. Who does?"

Reading multiple biographies of a single figure underscores the range of response that a fact or an event can inspire. In John Charmley's revisionist account *Churchill: The End of Glory,* he quotes from Churchill's address to the House of Commons on June 4, 1940:

> We shall go on to the end. We shall fight in France, we shall fight on the seas and oceans, we shall fight with growing confidence and growing strength in the air, we

shall defend our Island, whatever the cost may be. We
shall fight on the beaches, we shall fight on the landing
grounds, we shall fight in the fields and in the streets, we
shall fight in the hills; we shall never surrender.

Charmley admits that this speech, considered one of
Churchill's most inspiring and significant, was "sublime,"
but, he concludes, it was "sublime nonsense."

These examples illustrate the multiple interpretations and
characterizations that can be given even to simple facts, and
many issues are far more difficult. Was the Dardanelles strategy wrongheaded or brilliant—and how responsible was
Churchill for that military disaster? Was Churchill an aristocratic snob or a friend of the working class? Why was he
ousted as Prime Minister in 1945? Layers of facts refute one
another. And there's also the question of what facts matter.
For example, does a biographer emphasize incidents like
Tonypandy or Antwerp or Greece—or not? Explore
Churchill's sex life, his financial arrangements, his friendships, his diet, his religious beliefs—or not?

To make sense of the conflicting evidence, and to establish
what I thought important, I decided to write a biography of
my Churchill.

Churchill, of course, hasn't lacked biographers. About 650
biographies cram the shelves, and his official biography alone
runs eight volumes and more than nine thousand pages—the
Guinness Book of World Records ranked it the longest biography in English. Added to this are dozens of memoirs by his
friends, family, and colleagues; Churchill's appearance in

thousands of histories; and Churchill's many accounts of his own life.

Unlike that of his other biographers, my life didn't overlap Churchill's. Geoffrey Best, John Charmley, Martin Gilbert, Roy Jenkins, John Keegan, John Lukacs, William Manchester, Clive Ponting, Robert Rhodes James, Norman Rose, and all the others can remember the living Churchill, but I was born after he'd died. Churchill was never a presence in my life. I'm different in other ways, too: most of his biographers are British, and as far as I can tell, they're all men, except for a few friends and relatives.

I don't feel apologetic, as others have claimed to do, for writing another life of Churchill. There are many, it's true—even in 1950, Churchill said of his life to a biographer, "There's nothing much in *that* field left unploughed"—but each generation must retell his life, and not only as new facts emerge. "These facts are not like the facts of science—once they are discovered, always the same," observed Virginia Woolf, of biography. "They are subject to changes of opinion; opinions change as the times change." A biographer must get the facts right, but accuracy is not interpretation—and interpretation can never be final.

I could see a Churchill towering over the pages, vivid, brave, and tragic, and I wanted to describe this Churchill, *my* Churchill. As I did my research, I could feel myself skipping and lingering, careful not to discover too much in my scavenger hunt through history. Would I find only what I was looking for?

To cure this, I decided to write a biography that would

make my case for my Churchill but also press the opposing arguments—a biography that would convey the ambiguities of his character and reputation as well as the elementary themes of his life. Was he a great champion of democracy, or not? Was he an alcoholic, or not? I would present both arguments. That way, the biography could give the reader a perspective usually only gained by reading ten biographies, with their contrasting viewpoints.

To capture this complexity, I elected to portray Churchill by looking at him from multiple angles. And so *Forty Ways to Look at Winston Churchill* is both about Churchill and about the problem of giving an account of Churchill. It asks the reader to look at Churchill in multiple ways and, by doing so, to consider the problems inherent in biography.

This book is divided into forty chapters, each creating a different picture of Churchill. Why forty? Historically, *forty* meant "many"—just as we, after inflation, use the word *million*: "There are a million reasons to study Churchill." Because form is as influential as substance, *Forty Ways* exploits various structures, some quite unexpected, to tackle its subject. And rather than try to reconcile conflicting views, I've kept them distinct, so readers may decide for themselves what picture emerges.

There's a long tradition of reexamining the same subject in multiple ways: the four Gospels, Bach's *Goldberg Variations,* Wallace Stevens's "Thirteen Ways of Looking at a Blackbird," Kurosawa's *Rashomon,* and Monet's Haystack and Rouen Cathedral series all demonstrate the subtleties that emerge when a single subject is viewed under different lights. Dark and bright, blame and praise, must both be included: only one with a thorough knowledge of Churchill's character, even his faults, can appreciate his grandeur; only one who sees his inconsistencies can understand his hard core.

This multi-angle approach is meant to demonstrate biography's limits. A single biography, read alone, is almost always convincing; as Janet Malcolm observed, "The lay reader, who knows only what the biographer tells him, reads . . . in a state of bovine equanimity." The reader who continues to a second biography is more likely to question the facts. Katherine Anne Porter denied a biographer's ability to capture the truth when she wrote in the margin of a biography about herself, "Another bloody monkey mind! Can't you keep your grubby paws off of our lives. You don't know anything and can't guess right so shut up." By providing multiple interpretations, this biography means to reveal the unreliability of confident conclusions.

To distill Churchill's sprawling life into its essential elements, each chapter focuses on one question. What was Churchill's supreme moment? How did he see the world? What was his dominant quality? What were his motives, his formative role, his weaknesses, the important dates of his life? How did he look? How did he die? What made him a hero? Did he cheat on his wife? Such questions sound naive when put bluntly, but they are, after all, what we want to learn when we study great lives.

This fragmented approach seemed the most economical and also the most exciting way of pulling out the essential—

essential, to be sure, *in my view*—from the overwhelming material about Churchill's life. With so much eliminated, Churchill's themes emerge sharply: the Island and the Empire, the attraction of war, the craving for fame, the tears, the tension between the imagined and the real. I describe my Churchill—a hero, a genius, one of the greatest men who ever lived. But this biography also shows there are other Churchills.

And so this life of Churchill is irregular; it dwells on some topics and omits others. I have good precedent for my method. Churchill, whose lack of university education didn't stop him from writing biographies and histories, wrote of his *History of the English-Speaking Peoples,* "This book does not seek to rival the works of professional historians. It aims rather to present a personal view." Clement Attlee noted of that history, and the observation applies just as well here, that it could have been titled "Things in History which Have Interested Me." In this account are the things about Churchill which have interested me.

I hope that this biography—inconclusive as it is—will help others to catch a glimpse of Churchill's extraordinary character and life, and to consider, as well, how little we can know anyone, and how impossible is the task of summing up.

1

CHURCHILL AS LIBERTY'S CHAMPION

Heroic View

As their subtitles reveal, most of Churchill's biographers acclaim him as a hero: Isaiah Berlin's mystical tribute, A Portrait of a Great Man at a Great Moment; *Geoffrey Best's balanced praise,* A Study in Greatness; *Martin Gilbert's meticulous volumes, including* The Prophet of Truth *and* Finest Hour; *William Manchester's virile adventure story,* The Last Lion. *Memoirs like Violet Bonham-Carter's intimate portrait, Pug Ismay's loyal account, and Jock Colville's reminiscences argue the same case. And of course, of all the mythmakers, no one did more than Churchill himself to construct the heroic "Churchill."*

A torrent of facts proves their conclusions: that Churchill was a great man and the savior of his country; a farsighted statesman; a brilliant politician, orator, and writer; a loving husband and father; a man with a few endearing faults—or if not endearing, excusable.

Winston Churchill, June 1943.

No leader did more for his country than Winston Churchill. Brave, magnanimous, traditional, he was like a king-general from Britain's heroic past. His gigantic qualities set him apart from ordinary humanity; there seemed no danger he feared, no effort too great for his limitless energies.

Churchill's finest hour came in 1940. After warning for years against the Nazi threat, he rallied Britain to stand alone against Germany—after France and so many countries had fallen, and before the Soviet Union and the United States could be prodded into action. Churchill—with his tremendous gifts of eloquence, energy, and refusal to compromise and with his colorful symbols of cigar, whiskey, and V sign—became an icon of courage and liberty. In the greatest conflict in human history, which consumed the lives of 55 million people, Churchill alone saved England and the world.

But the famous triumphs of 1940 are just a small part of his story. Churchill burst into public life as a war hero and journalist and entered national politics at age twenty-five. Within a few years, he was a leading English figure—in fact, the first Churchill biography appeared when he was merely thirty-one years old. In his sixty-two years in the House of Commons, Churchill held every major government office, with the exception (ironically, given his tremendous influence in foreign affairs) of Foreign Secretary. This experience gave him an unparalleled grasp of the workings of Britain's civil and military machinery.

Churchill's abilities weren't exhausted by political administration. His voluminous writings and speeches were of remarkable quality and influence; he was an accomplished painter, a fast bricklayer, an airplane pilot, a polo player, and a crack shot; he was also a devoted husband and loving father.

The facts of Churchill's life are fabulous in their sweep—a pageant of English life. His earliest memory was of watching scarlet soldiers on horseback while his grandfather, the

Duke of Marlborough, addressed a crowd in Ireland. India, primogeniture, the trenches, Windsor Castle, silver trays, labor strikes, puddings, rose gardens, lions, umbrellas . . . all these weave through his story.

Winston Churchill was born on November 30, 1874. His father, Lord Randolph Churchill, was a gifted politician and a descendant of John Churchill, the first Duke of Marlborough and the greatest British general of the eighteenth century. His mother Jennie, a beautiful, accomplished American, was the daughter of New York financier Leonard Jerome.

From boyhood, Churchill had craved adventure, and in 1896, he sailed with the Fourth Hussars to India. There, restless with a cavalry officer's light duties, he pored over works by Macaulay, Gibbon, Darwin, Plato, and Aristotle, as well as records of parliamentary debates and his father's speeches, in a rigorous program of self-education. Impatient to make his name, to see action, and to earn money, Churchill also won assignments as a war correspondent. This began his career as a writer; over his lifetime, he would write acclaimed books about military campaigns he'd seen, biographies, histories, essays, and even a novel, as well as innumerable magazine and newspaper articles.

In 1899, Churchill set off to report from the Boer War, where he was captured during a brave attempt to rescue an armored train. He soon managed to escape and, as he stole across enemy countryside, happened by pure luck to knock at the door of a British-born coal-mine manager, who arranged his passage to safety. He received a hero's welcome, and the thrilling story of a Duke's grandson outfoxing the enemy made him a national celebrity.

But Churchill knew he wanted to be a politician, not a soldier. Back in England in 1900, he won his first election and entered the House of Commons as a Conservative at age twenty-five, as his father had done at the same age.

Because of his strong support for free trade, in 1904 Churchill switched from the Conservative to the Liberal Party. His talents shot him into prominence, and, already a Cabinet member at age thirty-three, he would go on to hold a remarkable array of offices. His tremendous abilities, force-fulness, and trenchant wit were acknowledged by everyone. In no time, Churchill made himself into an outsize public figure famous throughout Britain; he wasn't even thirty-five years old when Madame Tussaud's added his life-size wax figure to its displays.

In 1908, after a whirlwind courtship, he married Clementine Hozier, to whom he remained happily married for the rest of his life.

In his early Cabinet posts, Churchill helped build the foun-dation for the modern welfare state; then, in a move that marked a shift from domestic to military policy, he became First Lord of the Admiralty in 1911. Although his tenure there was among the most satisfying in his career, it ended in frustration.

During World War I, Churchill championed a daring plan to break the war's bloody stalemate by taking the Dardanelles Straits, which lie between the Turkish mainland and the Gallipoli Peninsula. By forcing the Dardanelles, the link be-tween the Mediterranean and the Black Sea, and by seizing

Constantinople, the capital of Britain's enemy, Turkey, the allies could ship supplies directly to Russia's Black Sea ports—and by helping the Russian armies, reduce pressure on the Western Front.

The War Cabinet approved Churchill's plan but failed to ensure sufficient support, and despite Churchill's monumental efforts to save the campaign, it failed. When the Liberal government fell, the Conservatives insisted on Churchill's ouster as a condition of coalition. Out of office, discouraged by his inability to contribute to the war effort, Churchill went to serve at the Western Front (no other politician of his stature served in the trenches). His war against lice, his improvements to conditions, and his fearlessness under fire won the admiration of his men. Too capable to be allowed to remain in the field for long, he returned to London in 1917 to take up a series of important positions.

After returning to the Conservative Party, Churchill ascended in 1924 to Chancellor of the Exchequer—a post second only to the Prime Minister. He'd nearly reached the summit of power.

In the "wilderness period" of the 1930s, however, the political tide turned against him. From the sidelines, he hammered against the menace of German rearmament and the policy of appeasing dictators, but for years, no one listened. Over time, though, as Hitler's treachery confirmed his predictions, Churchill's authority grew. He'd long urged a confrontation with Germany, and when Britain declared war, it was clear that Churchill must join the fight. He returned as First Lord of the Admiralty.

When Prime Minister Neville Chamberlain's government fell in May 1940, the nation turned to Churchill. At last his unique qualities were brought to bear on a supreme challenge, and with his unshakable optimism, his heroic vision, and above all, his splendid speeches, Churchill roused the spirit of the British people. Years later, Churchill recalled this time: "There was a white glow, overpowering, sublime, which ran through our island from end to end." Churchill lit that glow.

On June 16, 1940, France collapsed. Britain stood alone, under constant air attack and threat of invasion, while Germany controlled all of Europe. "Let us therefore brace ourselves to our duties," Churchill exhorted, "and so bear ourselves that if the British Empire and its Commonwealth last for a thousand years, men will still say, 'This was their finest hour.'"

On June 22, 1941, Germany invaded the Soviet Union, and Churchill immediately pledged British aid. On December 7, Japan attacked Pearl Harbor, and Britain declared war on Japan even before the U.S. Congress did. The three great Allies were then engaged, to fight to the end, despite their profound differences. Slowly, the Allies began to turn the tide, and after years of battle, Germany capitulated. On May 8, 1945, as Churchill announced victory in Europe, an enormous crowd gathered to cheer him. "In all our long history," he thundered, "we have never seen a greater day than this."

Churchill wasn't allowed to savor victory. Within weeks, to the shock of the entire world, he was voted out of office by a public determined to put memories of the war and its sacrifices behind them. With remarkable prescience, Churchill had observed in 1930: "The Englishman will not, except on great occasions, be denied the indulgence of kicking out the Ministers of the Crown whoever they are." In 1945, the British people showed him just how well he understood them.

On August 14, 1945, after two strikes by atomic bombs, Japan surrendered.

After the war, Churchill devoted himself to writing, but he wasn't content merely to comment on history. He continued to be an influence on foreign affairs and in March 1946, on a visit to the United States, gave his famous speech: "From Stettin in the Baltic to Trieste in the Adriatic, an iron curtain has descended across the Continent." The public called Churchill back to power in 1951, and he remained Prime Minister until old age finally halted him in 1955. He took leave of Queen Elizabeth, whose great-great-grandmother had reigned when he received his army commission.

Still active in retirement, in 1962, at age eighty-seven, he broke his hip while abroad. A French hospital prepared a bed for him, but he said, "I want to die in England." The Prime Minister sent a Royal Air Force Comet to bring Churchill back to London. Churchill kept his seat in the House of Commons, the institution he loved so much, until 1964.

Winston Churchill died on January 24, 1965, at age ninety, and in a rare honor, received a state funeral. Hundreds of thousands of people stood in line for hours to pay their respects to the man who'd done so much, in so many capacities, for his country. Afterward, his body was carried by train through the winter countryside to Bladon churchyard, where he'd chosen to be buried beside his father.

"We shall defend our Island, whatever the cost may be," Churchill had vowed in June 1940. "We shall fight on the beaches, we shall fight on the landing grounds . . . we shall never surrender." His service to his country will never be forgotten, and his words will be celebrated as long as the world rolls round.

2

CHURCHILL AS FAILED STATESMAN

Critical View

Laboring beside the Churchill mythmakers are the demythologizers, who challenge the heroic accounts by exposing a different set of facts. Clive Ponting, for example, emphasizes Churchill's reactionary, arrogant ideas; John Charmley argues that Churchill's unrealistic dedication to war and trust in the United States led to the collapse of British power; and David Cannadine amasses evidence of Churchill's many character flaws. Diaries and letters, such as those by Lord Moran and General Sir Alan Brooke, divulge Churchill's failings as an administrator, a strategist, and a colleague.

Together, these describe an opportunistic, antidemocratic, warmongering, spendthrift egotist who, with his obstinate belligerence and sentimental trust of the United States, fatally undermined the Empire.

Churchill was a crossbreed of English aristocracy and American plutocracy.

On his father's side, the Churchills were a textbook ex-

Winston Churchill, August 1944.

ample of a blue-blooded dynasty in decline. Though the Marlborough line was venerated, family members distinguished themselves mostly by debts, gambling, drinking, philandering, and scandal. Churchill's father Randolph shared many of these faults. He was a brilliant but unstable demagogue who rocketed his way to early political prominence and then threw away his career when, as Chancellor of the Exchequer, he resigned over a budget issue. He never held office again and died young and insane, likely from syphilis.

The family of Churchill's American mother, Jennie Jerome, was also inclined toward gambling, profligacy, and infidelity (Jennie was named after one of her father's mistresses, Swedish soprano Jenny Lind). Jennie escaped none of these undesirable family traits. She had numerous lovers, many of whom would be conscripted to boost her son Winston's career. Throughout her life, her extravagance would keep her on the brink of financial disaster.

Randolph and Jennie met on August 12, 1873, and married the following April. Winston was born only seven months later—according to the *Times,* prematurely, but not everyone believed that.

Too busy with their fashionable lives to take an interest in their children, Jennie and Randolph left their two sons mostly in servants' care. Churchill depended on his nanny Mrs. Everest—whom he called "Woom" or "Woomany"— for affection and attention. Already at boarding school at age nine, Churchill wrote his negligent mother, "It is very unkind of you not to write to me before this, I have only had one letter from you this term." When his parents did concern themselves with Winston, he disappointed them with school reports of tardiness, laziness, and misbehavior. He also lisped on the letter *s,* which gave his speech a slurred, unattractive sound.

His father arranged for him to go into the army—not out of any belief in Winston's military abilities but because he'd concluded his son wasn't clever enough to become a lawyer. Even so, Churchill twice flunked the entry exam for the military academy at Sandhurst and barely squeaked through after six months with a London "crammer." He qualified only for the cavalry—where, because financial demands on officers were greater, intellectual demands were lower than for the infantry.

Churchill's regiment arrived in India in 1896. Churchill had skated through school, but at this point he decided that to achieve the fame and power he craved, he must educate himself. In a crash course of self-improvement, Churchill read through an assortment of books sent by his mother. Throughout his life, he showed the undisciplined intelligence typical of autodidacts; he was incapable of rigorous analysis, and after making his conclusions, clung to them too stubbornly.

Over the next few years, Churchill schemed to join Britain's "little wars." He relished these battles: "This kind of war was full of fascinating thrills . . . at the worst thirty or forty, would pay the forfeit; but to the great mass of those who took part in the little wars of Britain in those vanished lighthearted days, this was only a sporting element in a splendid game." (The "fascinating thrills" were perhaps less obvious to those fighting the British. In the Battle of Omdurman, for example, British losses were 25 dead and 136 wounded; Muslim dervishes had 10,000 dead and 15,000 wounded.)

Churchill exploited every family connection to get himself posted to scenes of military action—so he could win fame either by performing heroic deeds or by writing about them. He soon appreciated that the quickest path to the limelight was to criticize the most prominent men, and he never shrank from telling others, including military superiors, how to do their jobs. One early book, *The River War*, was disparaged as "A Subaltern's Advice to the Generals."

In 1899, Churchill made his first campaign for a seat in the House of Commons—and suffered his first of many defeats. After losing, he retreated to South Africa to report on the Boer War and was almost immediately captured. Abandoning companions who'd planned to escape with him, Churchill bolted from the prisoner-of-war camp and fled to safety. With his instinct for the spotlight, Churchill exploited the potential of his escape. He telegraphed ahead with news of his adventure so he could be greeted with a hero's welcome, which he acknowledged with a well-prepared "impromptu" speech. As he'd planned, the press eagerly picked up the story.

Back in England, his carefully managed stature as a war hero helped him win election to Parliament (barely) in 1900. Churchill waited a mere four days after taking his seat to make his maiden speech; the *Daily News* reported that "address, accent, appearance do not help him."

Four years after being elected as a Conservative, he decamped to join the stronger party, the Liberals, which rewarded this desertion with an important appointment. Churchill would use the turncoat trick again, in 1924, to "re-rat" to the Conservatives when that party was again in power.

Although no one denied his intelligence, responsible people considered Churchill a reckless and conceited opportunist. Switching parties won him enemies each time, of course. He also infuriated colleagues in every position he held. He interfered in other people's responsibilities, exceeded the bounds of his authority, and failed to set sound priorities. He overworked his staffs and diverted them to work on his pet projects. "He was hated, he was mistrusted, and he was feared" was how even a close friend characterized Churchill's reputation. Even his own family disliked him. The dowager Duchess of Marlborough admonished the new wife of the ninth Duke: "Your first duty is to have a child and it must be a son, because it would be intolerable to have that little upstart Winston become Duke."

Churchill was a gifted speaker when properly prepared, but he couldn't think on his feet and rarely said anything in public he hadn't memorized. His speeches were plotted right down to stage directions—"pause; grope for word"; "stammer; correct self"—meant to give the impression he was extemporizing. Although his speeches read well today, he often failed to persuade his actual audiences because he couldn't adapt his prefabricated pieces to the mood of the situation.

Churchill made his career in Parliament but had some trouble with elections. When he lost in 1908, "What's the use of a W.C. without a seat?" was a joke that made the rounds. In 1922, Churchill lost and was rejected three times by the voters before he finally got himself elected in 1924.

Despite the widespread suspicion he aroused, and despite the elections he lost, Churchill managed to attain several high offices in the 1910s and 1920s. That period is dominated, however, by the debacle of 1915, when, as First Lord of the Admiralty, Churchill forced through his plans for the disastrous Dardanelles campaign. Unrealistic in his goals, unwilling to consider his colleagues' grave misgivings, Churchill pressed for commitment of British forces. The result: a catastrophic slaughter of troops that led to the fall of the government. Churchill loudly withdrew to the trenches on the Western Front but stayed fewer than six months—fewer than three months in frontline conditions. He soon managed to rejoin the government as Minister of Munitions, but the grim question "What about the Dardanelles?" would dog him for the rest of his life.

Consistency of policy was not Churchill's hallmark. Although in the 1930s Churchill would castigate the government for Britain's lagging military might, during the 1920s he himself worked to enfeeble British armed forces. As Secretary of State for War and Air, he cut Royal Air Force plans for 154 squadrons to a mere 24, and as Chancellor of the Exchequer, he fought to shrink defense spending. Also as Chancellor, in what he himself later called the "biggest blunder in my life," in 1925 Churchill ignited a monetary crisis when he returned Britain to the gold standard, a policy that led to deflation, unemployment, and industrial unrest.

Churchill supported a large family and a lavish lifestyle on his earnings, and as a result, his finances were always shaky. In 1929, he lost his savings in the Wall Street crash and kept out of ruin only through his efforts as a writer. Churchill's major works were all about himself, to greater or lesser extent—his personal experiences, his family, or at most remove, his view of his country. He churned out material and somehow managed to keep afloat.

From 1929 to 1939, shunned by Conservatives and Liberals alike, Churchill was excluded from executive office and influence. Much of his isolation was due to his vehement resistance to Indian independence; while most Britons supported a policy of gradual concession, he insisted that independence would mark the downfall of the British Empire and would reduce India to despotism.

Also during the 1930s, safe on the sidelines, Churchill had the luxury of criticizing the government's policies regarding Nazi Germany without having to grapple with the practical limitations of a tight budget, a weak economy, and pacifist public opinion. His grim warnings about Hitler were blunted by the lurid prophecies he'd made about the threat posed by Indian independence, by the Bolsheviks, by the trade unions, and by the "Socialists," as he called the Labour Party. His arguments about Germany were often ill informed—for example, he exaggerated German strength—and he proposed impractical measures. Nevertheless, Hitler's menace was real, and Churchill's position strengthened as the Nazi peril grew.

When Britain declared war on Germany, on September 3, 1939, Churchill joined the government as First Lord of the Admiralty. He became Prime Minister in May 1940, after the failure of the British operation in Norway—one for which, incidentally, Churchill bore most responsibility—led to the fall of Chamberlain's government. Many didn't want him as Prime Minister; his long-windedness, theatricality, ill judgment, habit of meddling, and also his heavy drinking, were notorious. However, Foreign Secretary Lord Halifax, the more favored candidate for Prime Minister, refused to accept the position, and so it settled on Churchill.

Once in office, to secure complete power and without seeking parliamentary approval, Churchill made himself Minister of Defense. Within two months, he controlled the government, the armed services, and Parliament. His friend and colleague Lord Beaverbrook admitted, "Churchill on the top of the wave has in him the stuff of which tyrants are made." Despite the enormity of his responsibilities, Churchill inserted himself into every process down to the size of the jam ration, misspellings in government telegrams, and the fate of bombed zoo animals.

All who knew Churchill agreed he was rude and egotistical. He interfered, he wasted time with his harangues and wild schemes, he refused to listen. Working with Churchill during the war, the Chief of the Imperial General Staff described him as "temperamental like a film star, and peevish like a spoilt child." In flagrant disregard of severe wartime rationing, Churchill smoked, drank, and ate to excess. Ordinary Britons were grateful for one egg and a few ounces of meat each week; Churchill's breakfast often exceeded a schoolchild's weekly protein consumption. At a time when George VI monitored the royal bathtub to limit hot water to five inches, Churchill's aide arranged for a back-up system in case of power outage at Chequers, to ensure that the Prime Minister wouldn't miss his daily hot bath, filled to the brim. Churchill's selfish habit of working late into the night—at times until 4:00 A.M.—exhausted those working around him. He raged at the typists who struggled to keep up with his torrent of words and rarely bothered to learn the names of his servants and secretaries.

Imagining himself to be the new Marlborough, weeping openly at patriotic scenes, proclaiming on the wireless, and most important, truckling to President Franklin D. Roosevelt, Churchill led Britain with little hope of victory until the entry of stronger nations, the Soviet Union and the United States, in 1941. Churchill and Roosevelt had a much-photographed "special relationship," but beneath the surface, Roosevelt opposed Churchill's reactionary ideas and doubted his enthusiasms. "Winston has fifty ideas a day," Roosevelt observed, "and three or four are good." He was also exasperated by Churchill's windy discourses. At one meeting, when Churchill began to speak, Roosevelt passed a colleague an irreverent note, "Now we are in for one-half hour of it."

As the war ground on, national support for Churchill changed to criticism. No one doubted his ability to inspire, but what about his other duties? In 1942, the *Tribune* asked bluntly, "How long can we afford a succession of oratorical successes accompanied by a series of military disasters?" The lack of a successor protected him. One officer noted that Churchill "is virtually dictator, as there is absolutely no one else to take his place. . . . I am sure [he] has a silent chuckle when he reminds the House that he is entirely their servant."

In time, however, Britain's allies shoved Churchill to the sidelines, and after 1942, effective direction of the war slid from his grasp. Churchill's sentimental trust in the United States, and in his friendship with Roosevelt, blinded him to the United States's determination to dismantle the Empire by forcing Britain to exhaust its wealth in the war effort and by requiring Britain to adopt pro-American trade policies.

Ignoring some of his wisest advisers, Churchill threw every possible resource into the war effort, and by doing so, he assured the British Empire's liquidation. The war's heavy human, financial, and material demands exacerbated the strain on the already overextended Empire to the point that, after the war, the depleted Britain could no longer stand as a great power.

Churchill refused to recognize the Empire's vulnerability. He also refused to acknowledge the changing mood in Britain—the spread of egalitarian feeling and the longing for peaceful prosperity. His ignorance of the people's hopes and his bitingly partisan campaign—as when he argued that British Socialists inevitably would use some form of "Gestapo"—offended the public. Two months after Germany's surrender, the British people voted Churchill out of office.

Two years later, Churchill lost a battle he'd considered one of the most important of his life, when Britain granted India its independence. Over the next few decades, the Empire would be dismantled; once India was gone, maintaining most of the rest of the British Empire in Africa and Asia was unnecessary and unworkable.

In 1951, at the age of seventy-seven and to the dismay of

his long-suffering heir apparent Anthony Eden, Churchill returned as Prime Minister. In June 1953, he had an incapacitating stroke, which, in a shocking deception, he hid from Parliament and the press. In 1955 he reluctantly resigned. He visited the House of Commons for the last time in 1964; he stayed only forty-five minutes and never returned. He died the next year, at age ninety.

During his life, Churchill had seen the Empire at its greatest, and, as he well recognized, he participated in its decline.

Mirroring his public life, Churchill's personal life was scarred by repeated failure. Three women rejected his marriage proposals before Clementine Hozier accepted him. Even Clementine considered backing out of the engagement, until her brother reminded her that she'd already broken off two engagements and that she couldn't humiliate a public figure like Winston Churchill.

Even in the earliest days of their marriage, Churchill made no attempt to hide his true priorities from his wife: he was talking politics with Lloyd George even before he and Clementine had left the church after their wedding ceremony. During their marriage, Churchill's relentless demands, extravagance, and disreputable associates drove Clementine to spells of depression. Eventually, she preferred not to spend too much time with her husband.

Most of Churchill's children didn't lead successful or happy adult lives.

His eldest daughter, Diana, born in 1909, wanted to be an actress but met with little success. She was twice divorced, suffered from depression, and died from a pill overdose in 1963.

Churchill's son, Randolph, born in 1911, was a journalist and failed politician. He was universally considered an overbearing, egotistical snob—in fact, one club's constitution stipulated, "Randolph Churchill shall not be eligible for membership." Drunken arguments, broken marriages, and unfulfilled ambitions marred his life.

Churchill's daughter Sarah, born in 1914, scandalized her parents first by going on the stage, then by marrying a vaudeville comedian, whom she soon divorced. She suffered from alcohol problems and unhappy romances.

His youngest daughter, Mary, born in 1922, had the most settled existence and lived with her family near her parents.

Of the solid virtues specially prized by the English—modesty, steadiness, dignity, composure—Churchill lacked all. He was loud, pushy, self-advertising; he thundered and wept. He worked hard but often fruitlessly. One historian noted, "Churchill stood for the British Empire, for British independence, and for an 'anti-Socialist' vision of Britain. By July 1945 the first of these was on the skids, the second was dependent solely upon America, and the third had just vanished in a Labour election victory." Churchill had a long career in British politics—in which all his greatest efforts failed.

3

CHURCHILL'S CONTEMPORARIES

Whom He Knew

Throughout his ninety years, Churchill crossed paths with the great or future great. This was partly the result of England's class distinctions, public-school network, and small, concentrated population; partly the result of the fact that Churchill had always been a man to meet. Even so, the astonishing range of his acquaintances illustrates the scope of a life that spanned many years (1874–1965) and many accomplishments. One person whom Churchill never met was Hitler.

Churchill Met:

Ethel Barrymore

Bernard Baruch

Cecil Beaton

Gertrude Bell

Irving Berlin

Isaiah Berlin

Rupert Brooke

Maria Callas

Austen Chamberlain

Joseph Chamberlain

Coco Chanel

Charlie Chaplin

Prince Charles

Chiang Kai-shek

Winston Churchill,
  American novelist

Kenneth Clark

Clark Clifford

Buffalo Bill Cody

Michael Collins

Noël Coward

Albert Einstein

Dwight Eisenhower

Margot Fonteyn

Greta Garbo

Billy Graham

Haile Selassie

Pamela Harriman (née
  Digby)

William Randolph Hearst

Alger Hiss

Herbert Hoover

İsmet İnönü

Henry James

Helen Keller

Grace Kelly

Joseph Kennedy

John Maynard Keynes

Rudyard Kipling

Lawrence of Arabia

Henry Luce

Somerset Maugham

André Maurois

Richard Nixon

Laurence Olivier

Aristotle Onassis

Emmeline Pankhurst

George Patton

John Profumo

Eleanor Roosevelt

Franklin D. Roosevelt

Theodore Roosevelt

Lord Rothschild

Vita Sackville-West

Siegfried Sassoon

Charles Schwab

George Bernard Shaw

Joseph Stalin

Adlai Stevenson

Tito

Harry Truman

Mark Twain

Consuelo Vanderbilt

Beatrice Webb

Chaim Weizmann

H. G. Wells

4

CHURCHILL'S FINEST HOUR—
MAY 28, 1940

The Decisive Moment

We search in a biography for the subject's decisive moment, the one that sums up a life's meaning or changes its direction. Churchill's life was starred with turning points: escaping from the prison camp, winning his first election, fighting for his reputation after the Dardanelles disaster, becoming Prime Minister, proclaiming victory in 1945, losing the election in 1945.

However, one period—the end of May 1940—stands out from the rest. It was at this dangerous time that Churchill showed himself most fully and used his gifts with greatest effect.

In a life crowded with dramatic moments, Churchill's most decisive hour fell in the late afternoon of May 28, 1940. He'd become Prime Minister just eighteen days before.

How had he got there? Though he'd made a spectacular start, his political career had sputtered to a halt over the last decade. Many in responsible positions considered him, how-ever brilliant, to be unreliable, erratic, a self-advertiser, a war-monger. The people as well as the government ignored his warnings about the Nazis: the British ruling class, he'd protested to no effect, continued "to take its weekend in the country," while "Hitler takes his countries in the weekends." Working against Churchill: pacifist sentiment rooted in World War I's destruction, belief that Germany had legitimate griev-ances, fear of the bomber, hope that a strong Germany would restrain Communism, and the weak British economy.

However, Hitler's actions proved Churchill's prophecies to be hideously accurate, and war erupted on September 3, 1939. That very day, Churchill returned as First Lord of the Admiralty, and when Chamberlain's government fell eight months later, Churchill became Prime Minister.

His premiership hadn't been a certain thing at all. Not Churchill but Lord Halifax, Foreign Secretary since 1938 and a proponent of appeasement, was the establishment's candidate to succeed Chamberlain. Churchill was a less ob-vious choice. Aged sixty-five, he qualified for an old-age pension. He was short, fat, and bald, with a forward stoop and jutting jaw. He drank constantly, cried frequently, painted pictures, didn't get out of bed until late morning, and recited poetry at the slightest encouragement. More signifi-cant, he'd made bitter enemies in his long parliamentary ca-reer. But at a small, quiet meeting on May 9, Churchill had been recognized as the man to lead the battle against Hitler.

Politically, he was weak. True, he'd supplanted Cham-berlain as Prime Minister, but Chamberlain was still the leader of the Conservatives, who dominated the House of Commons. Politically, Churchill had no choice but to include in his five-member War Cabinet two men, Chamberlain and Halifax, who had never believed in pursuing total war against Germany. Churchill hadn't yet proved himself in office, and his reputation—as a reckless adventurer—clung to him. Many predicted he wouldn't last long in office.

On the Continent, the Nazis had swept through Poland, Denmark, Norway, Holland, and Belgium, and on May 16, German troops pierced France's Maginot line. The French were fighting badly and losing hope; surrender would follow within weeks.

By the end of May, the British and French armies were trapped along the French coast at Dunkirk. Even the optimistic Churchill feared that perhaps only thirty thousand of more than three hundred thousand men could be saved. On May 26, the evacuation began. Some twenty miles of ocean, the narrow moat that protected the island from invasion, must be crossed by the British to bring their men to safety. Many—including American ambassador Joseph Kennedy—insisted that Britain couldn't survive.

While battle raged across the Channel, Churchill was fighting a fierce action within his War Cabinet. Although it had been Chamberlain whom Churchill had opposed for years, and whom he'd replaced, it was Halifax who proved his main adversary during his first days in office. Although no one then could have realized it, the decisive moment came on May 28, 1940.

In the days before, Halifax had argued that Britain would be "foolish" not to make peace, if terms could be reached that preserved its independence. His aim was to find a "decent" way for Britain to keep its Empire and fleet; he dismissed Churchill's hyperbolic resistance to exploring peace terms as "the most frightful rot." (Some historians, too, would later condemn Churchill for refusing to consider a compromise peace; the war's crippling cost, they argue, assured the Empire's collapse. Such critics don't explain why Churchill should have trusted Hitler, who could have returned to crush Britain once he'd dispatched Russia; or why Churchill should have viewed with composure a Nazi-controlled Continent; or how, in any event, Britain could have managed to continue its grasp on its vast, rebellious possessions.)

To keep Halifax, Churchill never flatly ruled out a compromise peace, but he didn't hide his own view that the only safety for Britain and France stood in endurance. He believed that any hint of British willingness to elicit a settlement proposal would wreck public morale and that the possibility of negotiation, once opened, couldn't be closed. The two men argued for several days, until their conflict reached its crisis on May 28.

Churchill was in a dangerous position. Across the Channel, prospects looked dire for British forces awaiting evacuation from Dunkirk. If these men couldn't be saved, Britain's hope of withstanding invasion was bleak. As for Churchill, the security of his political position depended on his former opponents. If Halifax resigned to protest

Churchill's policy, he would trigger a national crisis that would shake—and perhaps topple—Churchill's government.

At four o'clock, the War Cabinet met, and again, two visions of Britain's future confronted each other. Halifax urged consideration of a peace settlement. He feared—quite rightly, time would show—that without some limit to the conflict, Britain couldn't survive as a great power. Churchill believed that talks about peace terms were a "slippery slope" to capitulation. "Nations which went down fighting rose again," he declared, "but those who surrendered tamely were finished." With this crucial issue unresolved, the War Cabinet recessed for one hour.

What could Churchill do? He refused to countenance any compromise, but he couldn't risk an outright break with Halifax. So Churchill did what any embattled executive would do: he stacked a meeting.

During a break from the five-member War-Cabinet meeting, Churchill met with the twenty-five members of the full Cabinet. He explained the imminent troop evacuation, then he said "quite casually, and not treating it as a point of special significance: 'Of course, whatever happens at Dunkirk, we shall fight on.' " Churchill concluded:

I am convinced that every man of you would rise up and tear me down from my place if I were for one moment to contemplate parley or surrender. If this long island story of ours is to end at last, let it end only when each one of us lies choking in his own blood upon the ground.

He pretended to read, in these men's hearts, the determination that surged in his own, and the reaction was electric. The ministers—by no means all Churchill admirers—crowded around and cheered him. His vow—*whatever happens, we shall fight on*—and the Cabinet's support turned the weight of opinion. Halifax stopped his opposition. That day, Churchill issued a "strictly confidential" memo to remind his colleagues there was no place in his government for doubt or half measures.

> In these dark days the Prime Minister would be grateful if all his colleagues . . . would maintain a high morale in their circles; not minimising the gravity of events, but showing confidence in our ability and inflexible resolve to continue the war . . . whatever may happen on the Continent, we cannot doubt our duty, and we shall certainly use all our power to defend the Island, the Empire, and our Cause.

This was Churchill's hour to lead. His two predecessors—Stanley Baldwin and Neville Chamberlain—had had their virtues; but as with all qualities, these virtues took their color from circumstances. The very attributes that Baldwin and Chamberlain disliked in Churchill—his rashness, his simplicity, his buccaneer spirit—fitted him far better to events than did all their cool reasonableness. Churchill's vivid historical imagination allowed him to understand Hitler, while they clung to the illusion that Hitler was a statesman who operated by conventional rules.

Within a week Churchill would give his greatest speech.

On June 4, he spoke in the House of Commons, for little more than thirty minutes, about the extraordinarily successful evacuation of British troops from Dunkirk and concluded:

> Even though large tracts of Europe and many old and famous States have fallen or may fall into the grip of the Gestapo and all the odious apparatus of Nazi rule, we shall not flag or fail. We shall go on to the end. We shall fight in France, we shall fight on the seas and oceans, we shall fight with growing confidence and growing strength in the air, we shall defend our Island, whatever the cost may be. We shall fight on the beaches, we shall fight on the landing grounds, we shall fight in the fields and in the streets, we shall fight in the hills; we shall never surrender; and even if, which I do not for a moment believe, this Island or a large part of it were subjugated and starving, then our Empire beyond the seas, armed and guarded by the British Fleet, would carry on the struggle, until, in God's good time, the New World, with all its power and might, steps forth to the rescue and liberation of the Old.

Several Members of Parliament cried. So did Churchill.

Churchill's eloquence persuaded the British that their cause was worth every sacrifice, even death. "You can always take one with you" was one of his invasion slogans. The great theme of Churchill's life was *never surrender,* and he vowed he would lead his country to victory. So he did, but with what consequence, he never imagined.

5

CHURCHILL AS LEADER

Suited to High Office?

Winston Churchill Was Well Suited to High Office

Churchill's qualities made him an outstanding, inspiring leader, as demonstrated by his tremendous accomplishments in office.

One key to his success was his overwhelming energy. Abnormal energy coupled with power is a formidable force. Even detractors admitted he revitalized every office—First Lord, trench commander, Prime Minister—by the intensity of his personality. He drove others as hard as he drove himself.

Churchill was also able to grasp key facts without labored analysis. One aide observed that he "would read a long Cabinet Paper and pick out one or two aspects of the case, frequently those which did not seem the most important. . . . It was strange how often they turned out in the end to be the principal points at issue."

Churchill recognized the value of accountability and opposed efforts to add layers of advisers who lacked actual responsibility. "Lots of people can make good plans for winning the war if they have not got to carry them out," Churchill pointedly noted when he addressed a Joint Session of Congress in 1943. "I dare say if I had not been in a responsible position I should have made a lot of excellent plans."

Churchill saw things clearly, and he wanted others to share his vision: nothing in halftones or muted colors. During the confusion of war, he refused to allow muddle and drift to obscure what he saw: the tragic simplicity and grandeur of the times and issues at stake. Against the agonized compromises of the past, his certainty and his energy stood out in bright, bold relief. "You ask, what is our aim? I can answer in one word: It is victory." More than anything, his absolute conviction that Britain would triumph, and his ability to inspire his people to share his confidence, lifted the nation out of one of its darkest periods.

It was for these qualities that Churchill was hailed as the savior of his country.

Winston Churchill Was Ill Suited to High Office

Churchill was impulsive, disloyal, overbearing, eccentric, and as Dwight Eisenhower delicately admitted, he "rarely failed to inject into most conferences some element of emotion." He refused to respect priorities or lines of command, he interfered with commanders in the field, and he rarely listened to anyone. "All I wanted," he explained, only half joking, "was compliance with my wishes after reasonable discussion." He exhausted everyone around him with his late hours, cigar smoke, and endless monologues. He telephoned his staff at any hour of day or night, for any trivial reason. He usually worked on critical matters, especially important speeches, until the very last moment, which further strained those around him. At times, he could be extraordinarily persuasive, and he used this gift to win arguments he shouldn't have.

Churchill acted on impulse, not analysis. "Winston was never good at looking at all the implications of any course of action which he favoured," admitted General Sir Alan Brooke. "In fact, he frequently refused to look at them." He insisted on one-page answers to complex questions and showed no appreciation for practical difficulties. Churchill's lack of focus meant that, for one leading a world war, he spent an astonishing amount of time on trivialities. He found time in 1942 to write the First Lord to suggest that, in order to save the time of signalmen, cipher staff, and typists, signals should shorten the name of the ship the *Admiral von Tirpitz* to *Tirpitz*.

Churchill's inability to size up the public mood often undercut his effectiveness. For instance, he damaged his reputation by defending Edward VIII's extremely unpopular proposal to marry the twice-divorced American Wallis Simpson. Churchill's support of Edward also shows his inability to take the measure of others; later, the Duke of Windsor's sympathy for the Nazis led Hitler to comment,

"His abdication was a severe loss for us," and in fact, the Duke once hailed Hitler with the stiff-armed Nazi salute.

Churchill's zeal for the offensive distorted his judgment. He admired daredevils and undervalued those he considered too cautious, and this, along with his heedless combativeness, was a serious hazard during his whole career.

Because of these qualities, Churchill was an irresponsible and erratic leader.

6

CHURCHILL'S GENIUS WITH WORDS

His Greatest Strength

Biographies of great figures must tackle the essential question: what was the foundation of their genius? In Churchill's case, it was his extraordinary gift of expression. Perhaps it is possible for a leader to conceive large ideas without the ability to express them, but a leader unable to articulate such thoughts cannot inspire others to share them. Churchill was able to describe his timeless, heroic Britain so clearly that the entire nation rose to the level of his vision.

As soldier and statesman, Churchill had thrust himself into world events from age twenty-one, but, he pointed out, "Words are the only things which last for ever." Of all his accomplishments, it was his superb command of language that lifted him into triumph.

His words' power flowed from the fact that, without sounding insincere or affected, he could speak in both an arcane, heroic style and a plain, everyday style. Together these penetrated deeply into the public mind. During the Second World War, Churchill's words over the radio—whether in his own voice or read by someone else—were an essential source of the people's courage. Churchill recognized the significance of the new medium of radio, and he didn't grudge the massive effort needed to prepare his speeches.

The grand style was his hallmark. This wasn't bombast adopted for debate or broadcast, but how he naturally thought and spoke. His vocabulary had an anachronistic flavor, with words like *wickedness, parley, hardy tars, nay,* and *thrice.* He liked to use the bygone expression "pray," as in "Pray let me have a report"; this useful phrase was more commanding than "please" but less peremptory than "give me." He had his favorite words: *solid, squalid, unflinching, courageous, sultry, bleak, vast, grim, immense.* He enjoyed heaping adjectives together: Czechoslovakia was "silent, mournful, abandoned, broken"; Anglo-American relations would roll like the Mississippi, "inexorable, irresistible, benignant." But even with his ornate vocabulary, he had a gift for expressing himself so anyone could understand him.

During the war, Churchill's high style linked the present danger to Britain's noble history. He spoke the lordly language of heroes, of King Alfred, Queen Elizabeth, and Lord Nelson, returned from the past to encourage the people. After all, mixed in with their patriotic zeal, Britons worried about the mundane issues that dogged wartime existence: the blackout, the sugar shortage, the long line at the bus stop. Churchill inspired them to see their discomfort and fear as part of a glorious pageant.

Unsurprisingly, this grandiloquence irritated the more exact military or bureaucratic types. Churchill never shrank from introducing ideas that would usually have no place in the official world. In 1940, the King of Sweden sent George VI a message suggesting that peace possibilities be examined. On the Foreign Office's draft reply, Churchill admonished, "The ideas set forth . . . appear to me to err in trying to be too clever, and to enter into refinements of policy unsuited to the tragic simplicity and grandeur of the times and the issues at stake." His elaborate declaration of war on Japan struck some people as unnecessary flummery:

Sir,

On the evening of December 7th His Majesty's Government . . . learned that Japanese forces without previous warning . . . had attempted a landing on the coast of Malaya and bombed Singapore and Hong Kong.

In view of these wanton acts of unprovoked aggression . . . His Majesty's Ambassador at Tokyo has been instructed to inform the Imperial Japanese Government in the name of His Majesty's Government in the United Kingdom that a state of war exists between our two countries.

I have the honour to be, with high consideration,

    Sir,

        Your obedient servant,

            Winston S. Churchill

In response to critics, Churchill remarked, "Some people did not like this ceremonial style. But after all when you have to kill a man it costs nothing to be polite."

Churchill also made use of homely, everyday speech. "Short words are best," he said, "and the old words when short are best of all." His blunt sentences, with their colorful phrases, were as effective as his magniloquence. "I have nothing to offer but blood, toil, tears and sweat." "London can take it." "Never was so much owed by so many to so few." Often his most stirring lines were in simple language, as in his February 9, 1941, broadcast addressed to the United States:

> Put your confidence in us. Give us your faith and your blessing, and, under Providence, all will be well. We shall not fail or falter; we shall not weaken or tire. Neither the sudden shock of battle, nor the long-drawn trials of vigilance and exertion will wear us down. Give us the tools, and we will finish the job.

Churchill used words to bolster morale; he emphasized, for example, the importance of names. He intervened to improve the government's choices of names—an undertaking considered by many, no doubt, not to be the *most* effective use of his energies. It is easy to read his purpose: to make battles more glorious, weapons more menacing. He suggested the name "Mosquito Fleet" for a fleet of fast, small craft, then bettered it to "Hornet Fleet" or "Shark Fleet"—" 'Sharks' for short," he added. During the war's desperate first year, as volunteer defense forces mustered, he noted to the organizer, "I don't think much of the name 'Local Defence Volunteers' for your very large new force. The word 'local' is uninspiring. Mr. Herbert Morrison suggested to me to-day the title 'Civic Guard,' but I think 'Home Guard' would be better." Churchill prevailed.

Churchill also exploited the force of simile and metaphor. Of his opposition to socialism, he said, "We are for the ladder. Let all try their best to climb. They are for the queue." He wrote of a meeting with Roosevelt and Stalin, "There I sat with the great Russian bear on one side of me, with paws outstretched, and, on the other side the great American buffalo, and between the two sat the poor little English donkey who was the only one of the three, who knew the right way home."

Perhaps his most popular tool, whether in the House of Commons, in conversation, or with his wide readership, was humor, and one of his favorite techniques was anticlimax. Upon hearing that a captured German general was to eat dinner with the pompous Field Marshal Bernard Montgomery, Churchill confided, "I sympathize with General von Thoma. Defeated, humiliated, in captivity, and . . . dinner with General Montgomery." (He once characterized Montgomery: "Indomitable in retreat; invincible in advance; insufferable in victory.") Churchill was also master of the most British of comic devices, the understatement. Ringing church bells had been banned in June 1940, except to warn of imminent attack. In support of arguments that bell ringing should resume, Churchill admitted, "I cannot help feeling that anything like a serious invasion would be bound to leak out." He made hilarious, and devastating, use of sarcasm. Of the "courage" of one of his fellow MPs, he said, "First, it is that kind of courage which enables men to stand up unflinchingly and do a foolish thing, although they know it is popular. Second it is that kind of courage which cannot only be maintained in the face of danger, but can even shine brightly in its total absence." Even his talk of war could be funny. Of the June 1940 meeting at which the embattled French asked how Britain would resist invasion, Churchill wrote: "I said . . . my technical advisers were of opinion that the best method of dealing with German invasion of the island of Britain was to drown as many as possible on the way over and knock the others on the head as they crawled ashore."

One of Churchill's best targets for his humor was himself. In 1944, when asked not to repeat mistakes made after the First World War, he replied, "I am sure that the mistakes of that time will not be repeated; we shall probably make another set of mistakes." He made good fun of his French: in November 1944, he began a speech by warning: "Be on your guard, because I am going to speak in French, a formidable undertaking and one which will put great demands on your friendship with Great Britain." After the war, he addressed a French audience in English: "I have often made speeches in French, but that was wartime, and I do not wish to subject you to the ordeals of darker days."

Whether exploiting his lofty or common style, Churchill

was a brilliant writer. He produced innumerable articles, books, and speeches and threw off quotable lines in practically every conversation. Reading a newspaper account of an elderly man arrested for making improper advances to a girl, in icy weather, Churchill said, "Over 75 and below zero! Makes you proud to be an Englishman!" He'd been sharpening his rhetorical skills since his youth; although schoolmasters couldn't make him work, Churchill decided, in his twenties, that he needed an education. During the long, dull afternoons of army life in India, Churchill absorbed the works of Macaulay, Adam Smith, Darwin, Plato, and his greatest influence, Edward Gibbon's monumental *The Decline and Fall of the Roman Empire*. And he didn't merely learn by reading, but set himself to writing his own speeches on political events of earlier generations, to compare to what William Gladstone or Benjamin Disraeli had actually said.

Many people have been brilliant writers, and many people have been brilliant speakers. What distinguishes Churchill was his ability to rouse—and indeed, create—the dauntless Britain in which he believed.

Churchill denied that it was he who transformed the nation during the war. At the triumphant hour of May 8, 1945, Churchill cast the glory to the British people: *"In all our long history we have never seen a greater day than this."* At his eightieth birthday party a decade later, where he was called "the lion," he gave credit to the people: "It was a nation and race dwelling all round the globe that had the lion heart. I had the luck to be called upon to give the roar." In the same vein, a member of his wartime staff wrote, "His great speeches that thrilled the nation in 1940 expressed in matchless form what the men and women of Britain were feeling inarticulately."

That may have been true, but the men and women of Britain were "feeling inarticulately" many warring impulses. They felt defiant and courageous, yes. But they also felt fearful, confused, and desperate for peace. How many would have said they didn't want another war, or they didn't want to get mixed up in matters on the Continent, or they didn't care about fighting for the Poles or the Jews? At one of the most dangerous points in the war, just after he'd become Prime Minister, Churchill told the Cabinet, "If this long island story of ours is to end at last, let it end only when each one of us lies choking in his own blood upon the ground." The Ministers jumped up, shouted their agreement, rallied. But would they have said the same thing themselves, before Churchill had said it? Churchill found them courageous, but had conciliatory, peace-seeking Lord Halifax been Prime Minister, as many would have preferred, he might have discovered a very different mood. (Churchill once said, "Halifax's virtues have done more harm in the world than the vices of hundreds of other people.")

Many people don't know their own opinions until they hear them voiced by someone else. They're at the mercy of leaders, who, by articulating half-formed beliefs and fears, give them force. "The stronger man is right," said Hitler. Churchill said, "We shall never surrender." Churchill led the British people by reminding them of their history of liberty and courage; his courtly language conjured up their dead heroes. Hitler led the German people by giving voice to their fears, their ancient grudges, their cruel impulses, their rash eagerness for order and prosperity. Hitler told the Germans that they were a humiliated people, who would seize and destroy to gain their rightful first place; Churchill told the British that they were a valorous people, who would sacrifice everything in glorious defense of their island and of freedom.

Men are seldom more commonplace than on supreme occasions, wrote Samuel Butler. Churchill was a rare figure who rose to the level of events. He spoke the timeless speech of a hero, which he was; and also the daily talk of a common man, which he was as well. His power of expression was his greatest strength.

7

CHURCHILL'S ELOQUENCE

His Exact Words

With his genius for expression, Churchill could convey his ideas in phrases that burned themselves into people's minds. Eloquence matters: we cannot persuade others where we cannot voice our own thoughts. Decades after his death, Churchill remains one of the most frequently quoted figures in history.

Of a controversy that arose in 1894 about the proximity of bars to music halls, Churchill recalled: "I had no idea in those days of the enormous and unquestionably helpful part that humbug plays in the social life of great peoples dwelling in a state of democratic freedom."

In 1897, Churchill wrote: "Of all the talents bestowed upon men, none is so precious as the gift of oratory. . . . Abandoned by his party, betrayed by his friends, stripped of his offices, whoever can command this power is still formidable."

When Churchill was running for office for the first time, he went door to door to ask for votes. He knocked on the door of an irritable man who, when Churchill introduced himself, said, "Vote for you? Why, I'd rather vote for the devil!"

"I understand," answered Churchill. "But in case your friend is not running, may I count on your support?"

"I would rather be right than consistent."

As Undersecretary for the Colonies, in 1907, Churchill went to Africa with his private secretary, Eddie Marsh. After marching more than a hundred miles, he declared, "So fari—so goodie!" On the same trip, a colonial governor told him of the alarming spread of venereal disease. Churchill nodded, "Ah, Pox Britannica."

Before the first night of *Pygmalion,* playwright George Bernard Shaw wired Churchill: "Am reserving two tickets for you for my premiere. Come and bring a friend—if you have one."

Churchill replied: "Impossible to be present for the first performance. Will attend the second—if there is one."

"Success is going from failure to failure without loss of enthusiasm."

In a speech given in 1908, Churchill proclaimed:

Socialism seeks to pull down wealth, Liberalism seeks to raise up poverty. Socialism would destroy private inter-

ests—Liberalism would preserve private interests in
the only way in which they can be safely and justly preserved, namely by reconciling them with public right.
Socialism would kill enterprise; Liberalism would rescue
enterprise from the trammels of privilege and preference.

"Very few men are able to make more than one really bad
mistake."

When, in 1911, Churchill came under fire for his performance as First Lord of the Admiralty, he struck back by describing his critic as "one of those orators who before they
get up, do not know what they are going to say; when they
are speaking do not know what they are saying; and when
they have sat down, do not know what they have said."

"Megalomania is the only form of sanity."

"Perhaps it is better to be irresponsible and right than responsible and wrong."

"All newborn babies look like me."

On the problems of deploying a fleet during the First World
War, Churchill observed, "Out of intense complexities intense simplicities emerge."

Of World War I, Churchill wrote, "When all was over,
Torture and Cannibalism were the only two expedients

that the civilised, scientific Christian States had been able to deny themselves: and these were of doubtful utility."

In the 1922 election, the Liberals—and Churchill—suffered massive defeat. During the election, Churchill had his appendix removed, and he declared he awoke from his operation "without an office, without a seat, without a party, and without an appendix."

When Churchill met Hitler associate Putzi Hanfstaengel in Munich in 1932, he warned, "Tell your boss that anti-Semitism may be a good starter, but it's a bad sticker."

After touring the United States in the 1930s, Churchill was asked whether he had any criticism of America. He answered, "Toilet paper too thin! Newspapers too fat!"

Churchill appeared to be asleep in his seat in the House of Commons. "Must you fall asleep when I am speaking?" asked a fellow MP. "No," said Churchill, "it is purely voluntary."

"Nothing in life is so exhilarating as to be shot at without result."

A new barber asked Churchill how he'd like his hair cut. "A man of my limited resources cannot presume to have a hairstyle. Get on and cut it," answered Churchill.

In 1935, when Clement Attlee, then Lord Privy Seal, took a misstep and fell to the floor of the House of Commons, Churchill admonished: "Get up, get up, Lord Privy Seal! This is no time for levity."

When, in 1935, Anthony Eden was appointed Foreign Secretary under Baldwin, Churchill wrote Clementine: "I expect the greatness of his office will find him out."

"It is wonderful how well men can keep secrets they have not been told."

On November 12, 1936, as the Nazi threat grew, he spoke to the House of Commons on the subject of defense:

> The Government simply cannot make up their minds, or they cannot get the Prime Minister to make up his mind. So they go on in strange paradox, decided only to be undecided, resolved to be irresolute, adamant for drift, solid for fluidity, all-powerful to be impotent. So we go on preparing more months and years—precious, perhaps vital to the greatness of Britain—for the locusts to eat.

"There is never a good time for a vacation, so take one anyway."

In 1936, Churchill criticized Stanley Baldwin: "Occasionally he stumbled over the truth, but hastily picked himself up and hurried on as if nothing had happened."

"It is a good thing for an uneducated man to read books of quotation. . . . The quotations when engraved upon the memory give you good thoughts."

In 1938, a colleague compared Prime Minister Neville Chamberlain's attempt to convince Clement Attlee to support the Munich appeasement to a "snake dominating a rabbit." Churchill snorted, "It's more like a rabbit dominating a lettuce!"

"Never stand when you can sit and never sit if you can lie down."

In 1938, during a heated argument, his cousin Lord Londonderry, a pacifist, tried to drive home a point by asking, "Have you read my latest book?"
   "No," replied Churchill. "I only read for pleasure or profit."

Observing an elderly MP listening to Stanley Baldwin through an ear trumpet, Churchill asked, "Why does that idiot deny himself his natural advantage?"

"We seem to be very near the bleak choice between War and Shame. My feeling is that we shall choose Shame, and then have War thrown in a little later on even more adverse terms than at present."

"Where there is a great deal of free speech there is always a certain amount of foolish speech."

On October 1, 1939, in his first wartime broadcast, First Lord of the Admiralty Churchill observed, "I cannot forecast to you the action of Russia. It is a riddle wrapped in a mystery inside an enigma."

On the same day, in the House, Churchill declared about the heroic defense of Warsaw: "The soul of Poland is indestructible. . . . [S]he will rise again like a rock, which may for a spell be submerged by a tidal wave, but which remains a rock."

In October 1939, Churchill's twenty-eight-year-old son Randolph married nineteen-year-old Pamela Digby—because of the war, just weeks after their engagement. To those who said the couple couldn't afford to marry, Churchill replied: "What do they need?—cigars, champagne and a double bed." (Pamela Digby, later Pamela Harriman, would one day be the U.S. ambassador to France.)

In January 1940, in a BBC broadcast warning the neutrals of the consequences of not confronting Hitler, Churchill admonished: "They bow humbly and in fear to German threats of violence, comforting themselves meanwhile with the thought that the Allies will win. . . . Each one hopes that if he feeds the crocodile enough, the crocodile will eat him last."

At a dinner party, guests answered in turn the question, "If you could not be who you are, who would you like to be?"

When Churchill's turn came, he turned to Clementine and said, "Mrs. Churchill's second husband."

One evening in 1940, Churchill relaxed after dinner by tinkering with, then testing, a model bomb. He observed to a colleague, "This is one of those rare and happy occasions when respectable people like you and me can enjoy pleasures normally reserved to the Irish Republican Army."

With words uncannily matched to horrific events of later days, in 1940 Churchill broadcast to the nation about Hitler's bombing of London—on the resonant date of *September 11:*

> These cruel, wanton, indiscriminate bombings of London are, of course, a part of Hitler's invasion plans. He hopes, by killing large numbers of civilians . . . that he will terrorise and cow the people of this mighty imperial city. . . . Little does he know the spirit of the British nation, or the tough fibre of the Londoners . . . who have been bred to value freedom far above their lives. This wicked man, the repository and embodiment of many forms of soul-destroying hatred, this monstrous product of former wrongs and shame, has now resolved to try to break our famous Island race by a process of indiscriminate slaughter and destruction. What he has done is to kindle a fire in British hearts, here and all over the world, which will glow long after all traces of the conflagration he has caused in London have been removed.

In October 1940, discussing a general who was widely disliked, Churchill observed, "Remember, it isn't only the
good boys who help to win wars; it is the sneaks and the
stinkers as well."

Describing Hitler: "a haunted, morbid being, who, to their
eternal shame, the German people in their bewilderment
have worshipped as a god."

Before the war, Churchill had strenuously opposed Neville
Chamberlain and his appeasement policy. It was Chamberlain who, after meeting Hitler, decided "here was a
man who could be relied upon when he had given his
word." But once Churchill joined his government, he became Chamberlain's loyal servant, and he continued to treat
Chamberlain with courtesy after he'd replaced him as Prime
Minister. True, Churchill needed Chamberlain, but so often
a gloating victor refuses to put aside grudges and blame—
even in self-interest. Expediency alone doesn't account for
Churchill's magnanimity. When Chamberlain died in 1940,
Churchill gave a tribute to Chamberlain that honored his life
while acknowledging his mistakes:

> It fell to Neville Chamberlain in one of the supreme crises
> of the world to be contradicted by events, to be disap-
> pointed in his hopes, and to be deceived and cheated by a
> wicked man. . . . Whatever else history may or may not
> say about these terrible, tremendous years, we can be sure

that Neville Chamberlain acted with most perfect sincerity according to his lights and strove to the utmost of his capacity and authority, which were powerful, to save the world from the awful devastating struggle in which we are now engaged. . . .

Herr Hitler protests with frantic words and gestures that he has only desired peace. What do these ravings and outpouring count before the silence of Neville Chamberlain's tomb?

"Never give in, never give in, never, never, never, never . . . never give in, except to convictions of honor or good sense."

Despite repeated warnings from Britain and the United States, and in violation of the Nazi-Soviet Non-Aggression Pact, Soviet Russia was surprised by a German attack on June 22, 1941. For years, Churchill had denounced Communism, with its contempt for individual freedom, the rule of law, property rights, and the sovereignty of other countries. Churchill broadcast that night:

The Nazi régime is indistinguishable from the worst features of Communism. . . . It excels all forms of human wickedness in the efficiency of its cruelty and ferocious aggression. No one has been a more consistent opponent of Communism than I have for the last twenty-five years. I will un-say no word that I have spoken about it. But all this fades away before the spectacle which is now unfolding. The past with its crimes, its follies and its tragedies, flashes away. . . . Any man or state who fights on against Nazidom will have our aid.

In a lighter mood, he remarked, "If Hitler invaded Hell, I would make at least a favourable reference to the Devil in the House of Commons."

Churchill wrote of his emotions upon hearing that the Japanese had bombed Pearl Harbor in 1941:

No American will think it wrong of me if I proclaim that to have the United States at our side was to me the greatest joy. . . . Once again in our long Island history we should emerge, however mauled or mutilated, safe and victorious. . . . We might not even have to die as individuals. Hitler's fate was sealed. . . . As for the Japanese, they would be ground to powder.

In a speech given November 10, 1942, after Rommel's army was defeated, he said, "This is not the end. It is not even the beginning of the end. But it is, perhaps, the end of the beginning."

In November 1942: "The problems of victory are more agreeable than those of defeat, but they are no less difficult."

In 1943, to an American critic of the Raj, Churchill said, "Before we proceed any further, let us get one thing clear. Are we talking about the brown Indians in India, who have multiplied alarmingly under the benevolent British rule? Or are we speaking of the red Indians in America who, I understand, are almost extinct?"

In August 1943, for security reasons, Churchill was warned to keep secret how he was going to travel to the Quebec Conference. Talking to Canadian Prime Minister Mackenzie King, he said, "They won't let me tell you how I'm going to travel. . . . So all I can tell you is that I'm coming by puff-puff, if you know what I mean."

In January 1945, while waiting in Malta for President Roosevelt to arrive so they could proceed to Yalta for the Big Three conference, Churchill cabled Roosevelt: "No more let us falter! From Malta to Yalta! Let nobody alter."

On May 1, 1945, Hitler's death was announced. When asked in the House of Commons if he had any comment on the war situation, Churchill replied blandly, "It is definitely more satisfactory than it was this time five years ago."

On July 26, 1945, Churchill was voted out of office. When his wife tried to comfort him by saying, "It may be a blessing in disguise," he replied, "Well, at the moment it's certainly very well disguised."

In a speech in the House after the Potsdam Conference, Churchill observed, "There are few virtues which the Poles do not possess—and there are few errors which they have ever avoided."

In 1945, when invited to send Stanley Baldwin a birthday message, Churchill made a devastating refusal: "I wish Stanley Baldwin no ill, but it would have been better for our country if he had never lived." (It was Baldwin who, after Hitler invaded the Rhineland, refused to appoint Churchill as Minister of Defense because "If I pick Winston, Hitler will be cross.")

"The socialist dream is no longer Utopia but Queuetopia."

On August 9, 1947, he commented on the Labor government: "The Island is beset by a tribe of neurotic philosophers who, on awakening, begin each day by thinking what there is of Britain that they can give away, and end each day by regretting what they have done."

"Give to me the romance of an eighteenth-century alley with its dark corners, where footpads lurk."

When an aide returned one of Churchill's memos with a note correcting a sentence that he'd ended with a preposition, Churchill wrote his own note in return: "This is the sort of pedantic nonsense up with which I will not put."

To the House of Commons on November 11, 1947, Churchill observed: "No one pretends that democracy is perfect or all-wise. Indeed, it has been said that democracy is the worst form of Government except all those other forms that have been tried from time to time."

Asked whether he was flattered by the crowds drawn by his speeches, Churchill replied, "It is quite flattering, but whenever I feel this way I always remember that, if instead of making a political speech, I was being hanged, the crowd would be twice as big."

In 1953, of an unpromising candidate proposed for a peerage: "No, but perhaps a disappearage."

In 1954, when Clementine tried to put him on a restricted tomato diet, Churchill wrote, "I have no grievance against a tomato but I think one should eat other things as well."

In 1955, still firmly in office at age eighty to the consternation of his would-be successor Anthony Eden, Churchill said, "I must retire soon. Anthony won't live forever." He also observed, "When I want to tease Anthony, I remind him that Mr. Gladstone formed his last administration at the age of 83."

8

CHURCHILL IN SYMBOLS

Metonymy

It isn't enough that a biography explain what a person has done; it must explain how he or she was able to do it. During his life, and even after it, in the thickening haze of distance, Churchill kept his bulky figure fixed in people's view. He had a genius for presenting himself so he could be understood and remembered by everyone. How did he do it?—through symbols.

To drive himself into the public mind, Churchill simplified himself. As his image multiplied, it became more recognizable, as not only his appearance but even his character was reduced to a few swift strokes.

What makes certain bold figures stand out in the crowded bus of history? Churchill recognized that the public needs to see its heroes clearly. "One of the most necessary features of a public man's equipment," Churchill noted, "is some distinctive mark which everyone learns to look for and to

The uniform, the cigar, and the V sign make Churchill an instantly recognizable figure.

recognize." Like Hitler's toothbrush mustache, Montgomery's beret, or T. E. Lawrence's Arab robes, Churchill used his V sign, his cigars, his champagne and whiskey to blaze himself on the public mind. Just as his lisp and his idiosyncratic pronunciation made his voice identifiable on the radio, his distinctive appearance made him easy to recognize.

Early on, he'd used eccentric hats as one of his marks, and they were a constant subject of photographs and commentary. Later, he replaced hats with cigars: he was never without one. The cigar was a prop that gave him an air of manly nonchalance in a time of danger, of sensual pleasure at a time of austerity, and of jolly indifference to warnings about health or foreign protocol. Churchill was so closely associated with cigars that when he visited Roosevelt after the Pearl Harbor attack, map pins showing the location of the "Big Three" leaders were in the shapes not of flags or initials or even of a lion, an eagle, and a bear but of a cigar, a cigarette holder, and a briar pipe.

Churchill's characteristic gesture, the V sign, showed his skill at evoking emotion. Simple and memorable, it made a terrific contrast to the Nazis' sinister *Heil Hitler*. The V sign was suitably hostile: with the front of the hand toward the audience, as Churchill did it, it meant "Victory," but by turning the back of the hand to the audience, especially with an upward movement, the gesture became an obscene "Up yours!" It was also a call-and-response gesture that the crowd could use to signal their own confidence in victory. Leslie Hore-Belisha admitted of Churchill's hats and cigars, "Perhaps such foibles call attention to himself. But," he continued, "what of his V-sign? There we have his knack of evoking a patriotic emotion. It is a gesture of genius."

Casual of his public dignity, Churchill regularly wore a sort of zip-up coverall designed for air raids, which he called a "siren suit." The siren suits made for Churchill were sewn from different materials like worsted, pinstripe flannel, even black velvet for dinner, and some sported a large breast pocket to hold his cigars. Churchill's friend Diana Cooper described the effect: "Winston dresses night and day, and I imagine in bed, in the same little blue workman's boiler suit. He looks exactly like the good little pig building his house with bricks." Churchill, who loved to wear uniforms of all sorts, made the siren suit his signature garment. It first appeared in November 1940, and less than a year later, journalist H. V. Morton observed that it was "already acquiring a definitely historical appearance" and was "clearly destined for a glass case in years to come." The siren suit, Morton added with some cheek, made Churchill "seem rounder, plumper and more of a character than ever."

Although using these visual emblems—what renowned cartoonist David Low called "tags of identity"—may seem crude, the public embraced them. This was in a time, after all, before television made politicians' faces ubiquitous. Churchill's peculiarities sharpened his image in the public mind and also, given the English affection for eccentrics, boosted his popularity. And not only the British appreciated Churchill's symbols. When he spent Christmas in the White House, the gifts that poured in for him included a six-foot-tall V sign made of flowers and hundreds of boxes of cigars. Churchill was so closely identified with the cigar and V-for-victory sign that a birthday card that bore no address—just a drawing of a cigar between fingers giving the V sign—nevertheless reached him.

From the beginning of the war, Churchill exploited radio, and as the war dragged on, he increasingly relied on film as well. Newsreels allowed him to project himself through symbols to large audiences, without the exhausting preparation that a speech required. "His sensitiveness to effect was shown by various small traits of behavior," explained Sir John Martin, "presenting the character which the public expected and wanted to see—the hat, the stern set of the jaw, the cigar."

And Churchill exaggerated aspects not only of his appearance but also of his disposition. People feel closer to public figures when they can identify with their likes and dislikes, whether fishing, golf, broccoli, or as in Churchill's case, liquor. Churchill used his legendary drinking as a running joke that everyone could appreciate. Once, when asked if he'd like tea, Churchill replied, "My doctor has ordered me to take nothing non-alcoholic between breakfast and dinner." (But then he finished only two drinks all day.) Defending his request to his doctor to drink alcohol after lunch, Churchill explained, "I neither want it nor need it but I should think it pretty hazardous to interfere with the ineradicable habit of a lifetime."

"To be great," Clementine reminded Churchill, "one's actions must be understood by simple people." Churchill used symbols to press himself on the minds of the people. Whatever they thought about him, the British saw Churchill very clearly. As time passes, the clarity of these symbols helps to keep Churchill in sight while other immense figures—think of Joseph Stalin—begin to fade.

9

CHURCHILL, TRUE

In a Single Word

Many have tried to distill Churchill's character into a single word. "Liberty," one proposed; others suggested "courage," "persistence," "his fearlessness both physical and mental," "his vivid imagination," his "capacity for picking out essential things." British writer C. P. Snow, in a Churchillian series of powerful adjectives, described him: "Massive, witty, inconsiderate, he was sufficient for himself."

But it was Margery Allingham who best captured Churchill's character and his bond to the English. In a definition so forceful it bears reading at length, she summed up Churchill's character in a single word: true.

In 1941, to woo American support for Britain, the mystery writer Margery Allingham wrote *The Oaken Heart,* a book describing the wartime situation of her Essex village, called Auburn. Allingham explained how England responded to Churchill as Prime Minister and indeed explained so clearly that she foreshadowed, in 1941, his shocking defeat four years later.

Allingham began with a line from Shakespeare's *King John*:

"Naught shall make us rue, if England to itself do rest but true."

That is the basic rock, the ultimate secret belief of the instinctive Briton, the touchstone, the magic ring, the root of his pride, the cornerstone of his remembered history.

"Resting true" means what it says, too. It is not only resting honest, according to one's own or anyone else's lights. True means true. True as a line or a weight or a wheel is true, true like a ship's compass or a horseshoe or a gunsight. . . .

Mr. Churchill saved the government and saved the country and saved Auburn too. In a week it was over and all was safe and true again, whatever the outward danger. . . .

It is believed by some less simple people that Mr. Churchill, after having been neglected for years, was suddenly remembered in the hour of stress. Auburn does not see it in that way at all, as far as I can gather. From Auburn's point of view . . . Mr. Churchill has been perfectly recognized and liked and trusted to be true to himself and faithful to his country ever since he first appeared in Parliament. However, never until now has the country come into line, come into the true, that is, with Mr. Churchill. He is not a man to rise to an hour. The hour has had to rise to him. His is a fixed compass. The Auburn kind has always enjoyed him and known him as they knew his father and mother before him, and his tremendous qualities and tremendous peculiarities are not only known but understood by the people . . . and that is for a very good reason indeed.

Mr. Churchill is the unchanging bulldog, the epitome of British aggressiveness, and the living incarnation of the true Briton in fighting. . . . Moreover, he always has been like this as far as anybody remembers, and his family before him. After half a century the country has got into the true with him, but it is its fighting not its normal angle.

10

CHURCHILL'S DESIRE FOR FAME

His Motive

Although it is impossible to prove a subject's motives, a biography must probe them, because motive helps to explain a subject's actions. Why did Churchill do what he did? To maintain the Empire— because he loved war—to prove himself to his father. These theories are plausible, but there is another possible explanation as well: to satisfy his overpowering desire for fame.

Churchill was driven by his longing for fame. He lusted for honors, medals, offices, the respect of kings, a place in history. He worked constantly to thrust himself into the supreme role he believed he deserved. "What an awful thing it will be if I don't come off," he fretted as a junior officer. "It will break my heart for I have nothing else but ambition to cling to."

Growing up, Churchill watched his family members bask in public admiration. One of his grandfathers was the noble

Duke of Marlborough; the other was the millionaire "King of Wall Street." During Churchill's most impressionable years, his father Randolph was a star politician, a figure pointed out on the street, his speeches reported in full in the newspapers. In 1885, Churchill wrote his father from school, "Every body wants to get your signature will you send me a few to give away?" His mother Jennie was a celebrated society beauty whose photograph sold briskly in the shops during the 1880s and 1890s. What's more, Churchill claimed a national war hero—the first Duke of Marlborough—as an ancestor. From his family, Churchill learned early to crave fame for himself. At Harrow, when one of the senior boys beat him for breaking a school rule, Churchill boasted, "I shall be a greater man than you." "You can take two more for that," the boy replied. Even in those days, as a schoolboy, Churchill bragged about how important he'd be one day: "in the high position I shall occupy, it will fall to me to save the Capital and save the Empire."

Churchill spun a myth that he'd been ignored as a child, that he was always a dunce in school, and that he was hampered by a limited education. In truth, he brazenly capitalized on his aristocratic and political relationships. In particular, he goaded his mother to exploit all her connections for the benefit of his career. Practically no member of Britain's inner circle was beyond the determined reach of mother and son.

From his first days as a subaltern, Churchill sought the spotlight, and in fact, it was his desire for fame that explained his eagerness to be a soldier: "having seen service with

British troops while still a young man must give me more weight politically . . . and may perhaps improve my prospects of gaining popularity with the country." Polishing his reputation was always Churchill's first priority. Writing his mother in 1897, he complained that no one had noticed when he'd dragged a wounded soldier to safety: "given an audience there is no act too daring or too noble. Without the gallery things are different."

Like his father, Churchill had an instinct for grabbing public attention. He knew it wasn't enough merely to thrust himself into the center of the action—he must also make himself conspicuous. Churchill cultivated his remarks and appearance, with his cigars, hats, and gestures, to make himself irresistible to the newspapers. If his contrivances struck many as vulgar, if his blatant self-promotion added to his reputation for wild judgment, he didn't care. From his early days in India, when his ambitions were taking shape, he warned Jennie, "If I am to do anything in the world, you will have to make up your mind to publicity and also to my doing unusual things. Of course a certain number of people will be offended."

Churchill was right. A number of people *were* offended by his naked ambition, but rather than inhibiting him, this encouraged him. He embraced the label of troublemaker because he knew that the quickest route to fame was to criticize his most prominent colleagues. He whipped up strife because he knew that being the object of attack made him a larger figure. He twice made the controversial decision to change parties. Churchill used great causes—tariffs, social

welfare, the status of Ireland and India, the defeat of the
Nazis—as the ropes by which he hauled himself to prominence. He was in a hurry to beat out everyone else: early on,
he confided to a young dinner partner, "I am thirty-two already. Younger than anyone else who *counts,* though." His
personal ambitions, he admitted, were "an ugly and unsatis-
factory spectacle by themselves, though nothing but an advantage when borne forward with the flood of a great
outside cause."

Churchill's love of fame explains his unseemly gusto for
war: war always brought him new opportunities to thrust
himself into view. Of Churchill's ouster from power during
World War I, Frances Stevenson's diary noted how painful it
had been for Churchill to be absent from "the war to which
he had been looking forward all his life." Churchill loved the
showy trappings of war: the uniforms, which he wore whenever possible; the brass bands; the medals; the troops standing at attention. Because of his high position, World War II
gave Churchill the widest scope to indulge his appetite for
military pomp and ceremony. He related with glee that during his U.S. travels, the American press accorded his movements the same secrecy as the whereabouts of American
battleships. An official at the Tehran Conference commented
dryly on the extravagant number of generals, admirals, and
air marshals who accompanied Churchill, solely to make the
Prime Minister appear more grand. For those who didn't
share Churchill's attitude, his enthusiasm for war was alarming. As one colleague pointed out, "I thought that he was

nearly always right. . . . But I did think that he rather enjoyed a war: and, after three years in the infantry, in Gallipoli and France, I did not."

Churchill acknowledged that, in writing his novel *Savrola,* he gave voice to his own philosophy through his hero. On the desk in Savrola's library (which contains many of Churchill's own favorite volumes) rests Macaulay's *Essays,* with a passage marked by Savrola: "And History, while for the warning of vehement, high, and daring natures, she notes his many errors, will yet deliberately pronounce that among the eminent men whose bones lie near his, scarcely one has left a more stainless, and none a more splendid name." Savrola's craving for fame was also Churchill's.

11

CHURCHILL AS DEPRESSIVE

The "Black Dog"?

Winston Churchill Suffered from the "Black Dog"

Churchill himself spoke freely about his "black dog," as he called depression. In 1944, he reminisced to his doctor: "When I was young . . . black depression settled on me. . . . I don't like to stand by the side of a ship and look down into the water. A second's action would end everything."

The black dog appeared several times during Churchill's life. In July 1911, he wrote Clementine about a doctor who had cured an acquaintance of depression. "I think this man might be useful to me—if my black dog returns. He seems quite away from me now—it is such a relief. All the colours come back into the picture." He fell into depression after he left the Admiralty in May 1915, under the shadow of the

Dardanelles disaster and his subsequent fall from office. Clementine recalled it: "The worst part of our life together was the failure of the Dardanelles expedition. Winston was filled with such a black depression that I felt that he would never recover from it, and even feared at one time that he might commit suicide." During this time, the artist Sir William Orpen was painting Churchill's portrait. One day, Churchill arrived at Orpen's studio for a sitting but did nothing but sit in front of the fire with his head in his hands, without speaking a word. Orpen went to lunch and returned to find that Churchill hadn't moved.

The black dog reappeared during the 1930s, when Churchill was out of office, after his defeat in the election of 1945, and after his final resignation as Prime Minister in 1955.

Churchill's close friend Lord Beaverbrook described how Churchill alternated in mood between being "at the top of the wheel of confidence or at the bottom of an intense depression." Psychiatrist Anthony Storr, in an essay about Churchill's "black dog," based largely on an account written by Churchill's doctor Lord Moran, points out that depression is often inherited; the first Duke of Marlborough and Churchill's father Randolph both suffered recurrent bouts. Storr also argues that Churchill's very productivity proved depressive tendencies—that Churchill, fearful of falling into despondency, denied himself rest or relaxation. Churchill certainly kept himself feverishly busy at all times: with official responsibilities, writing, painting, bricklaying, polo, gambling, hunting, flying.

Winston Churchill Did Not Suffer from the "Black Dog"

Churchill didn't suffer unusually from depression. In distinguishing his life's unhappiest period—his school days—Churchill described himself: "I was happy as a child with my toys in my nursery. I have been happier every year since I became a man." He took voluptuous pleasure in champagne, cigars, and sunshine; in his large, noisy family; and in his passion for politics, writing, and painting.

The "black dog" notion stems chiefly from Churchill's doctor, Lord Moran, who wrote a valuable, but also widely disputed, memoir about Churchill. From his role as doctor, and with a deep interest in psychology, Lord Moran viewed his patient with a self-centered emphasis on the medical and psychological. Although Moran's book title claims that it was "taken from the diaries of Lord Moran," the eminent Churchill biographer Martin Gilbert has established that Moran's account was not based on a true diary. Contrary to Lord Moran, Gilbert concluded that while Churchill did show anger and sorrow in appropriate circumstances, he did not show signs of incapacitating depression.

Churchill did endure periods of despair—for example, after the military disaster at the Dardanelles. "I thought he would die of grief," Clementine said. But who wouldn't have felt that anguish? British troops had been devastated to no purpose. Churchill had been demoted to a position without influence. His reputation, as he rightly recognized, was permanently tainted. A spell of hopelessness would seem perfectly fitting. Over the next decades, during his tumultuous career, he would suffer several more very low periods. Debilitating bouts of depression, however, didn't mar Churchill's life.

12

CHURCHILL'S DISDAIN

His Dominant Quality

Often, in a large personality, a single exceptional quality pervades both faults and virtues, and the diligent reader of biography searches for this link, which, once found, will explain the subject's failures and successes, friendships and wardrobe. In Churchill, this quality was obvious: his disdain for other people's opinions.

Throughout his life, Churchill was indifferent to the opinions of other people, a maddening quality that gave him both his absurdity and his grandeur. "Of course I am an egotist," he said without apology. "Where do you get if you aren't?" Churchill gave no thought to other people's concerns and didn't hide his lack of interest in anyone but himself. He'd walk into the House of Commons, make a speech, and then walk out again without waiting to hear anyone else.

As the grandson of a Duke, a product of the Victorian age, and a world statesman, Churchill gave almost no thought to the convenience of his colleagues or servants. His secretaries worked every day except Christmas. Once, after arguing with his personal attendant, Churchill complained, "You were very rude to me"—to which the attendant retorted, "Yes, but you were rude too." Churchill thought this over and excused himself, "Yes, but I *am* a great man." During the frantic early days of the war, an aide typed a mock minute:

Action this Day

Pray let six new offices be fitted for my use. . . . I will inform you at 6 each evening at which office I shall dine, work and sleep. Accommodation will be required for Mrs. Churchill, two shorthand typists, three secretaries and Nelson [his black cat]. There should be shelter for all and a place for me to watch air-raids from the roof. This should be completed by Monday. There is to be no hammering during office hours, that is between 7 A.M. and 3 A.M.

W.S.C.

31.10.40

Churchill's staff didn't question the fake memo's authenticity.

Most taxing on those around him was his idiosyncratic schedule. He awoke about 8:00 A.M. and for hours worked and received visitors in bed. Then his ever-present valet helped him dress. After lunch, he napped for at least an hour. This was no furtive snooze—"no half-way measures," Churchill said; "take off your clothes and get into bed." At 8:30 P.M., dinner was served, and at about 10:30 P.M., Churchill went back to work. To the discomfort of his staff—who didn't share the luxury of being able to nap whenever they pleased—these were his prime working hours. He and his exhausted aides finally went to bed sometime between 2:00 and 4:30 A.M. Once asleep, Churchill left strict orders that he wasn't to be disturbed until 8:00 A.M., except in the case of actual invasion. In fact, on the morning of June 22, 1941, Churchill's aide didn't wake him until the usual hour—not even to deliver the staggering, welcome news that the German armies had invaded *Russia*. But although he himself hated to be interrupted while eating or sleeping, he thought nothing of disrupting anyone else's meal, sleep, or bath.

Self-important people are unconsciously funny. One observer recalled, "He dressed and marched around the room. . . . He is full of the poor whom he has just discovered. He thinks he is called by Providence—to do something for them. 'Why have I always been kept safe within a hair's breadth of death,' he asked, 'except to do something like this?' " When he left the Admiralty to become Prime Minister, he sent a melodramatic message to all Royal Navy personnel: "I shall not be far away." His histrionic gestures could be seen as heroic—or bathetic.

On many issues—such as Edward VIII's abdication, independence for India, and the planning for postwar reforms—Churchill's disdain deafened him to the public mood. "I'm quite satisfied with my views on India, and I don't want them disturbed by any bloody Indian," he said, when a colleague suggested he update his views on India by talking to some actual inhabitants of that continent.

Because he wasn't interested in other people, Churchill's conversation was usually one-sided. He dominated the talk and didn't bother to hide his boredom when anyone else took a turn. One hostess mocked him: "Winston leads general conversation on the hearth rug addressing himself in the looking glass—a sympathetic and admiring audience." Churchill talked for his own amusement, and to persuade others, and to wear them down from sheer exhaustion. Prime Minister Chamberlain explained that he'd left Churchill out of the Cabinet because he knew that, once there, Churchill wouldn't give anyone else a chance to get a word in. Dwight Eisenhower put it more tactfully: "He could become intensely oratorical, even in discussion with a single person." Not even President Roosevelt, on whom Churchill lavished as much charm as he possessed, escaped his late-night monologues—which, an aide admitted, Roosevelt sometimes found "tedious."

Every characteristic draws others along with it. Churchill's disdain for others' opinions gave him a quality of naturalness that bordered on the absurd. He worked each morning, visited by colleagues and secretaries, in a four-poster bed with flowery chintz hangings. He thought nothing of appearing in his favorite gaudy robe embroidered with scarlet dragons or being watched as he waltzed himself around the middle of a room. General Sir Alan Brooke described a meeting at the Churchillian hour of 3:00 A.M.: "[I]n his many coloured dressing gown, with a sandwich in one hand . . . he trotted round and round the hall giving occasional little skips to the time of the gramophone."

Even in public, Churchill could be careless of his dignity. He wore his siren suits whenever he felt like it and often looked both conspicuous and inappropriate—as when he insulted Soviet leaders by wearing one to a formal dinner at the Kremlin. He didn't care: he was Winston Churchill. He'd always been that way. As a schoolboy at Harrow, where open affection was much scorned, he'd kissed his nanny, Mrs. Everest, in full view of the other boys—a gesture described by war veteran Jack Seely as one of the bravest acts he'd ever seen. As a world statesman, to onlookers' astonishment, he was no different. Arriving in France during the "Phony War," he explained to a group of officials his predicament. "As there was a war on," he had decided to travel without his valet, which he hadn't done in twenty years. "To my surprise," he admitted without reserve, "I found I had no difficulty at all in shaving, brushing my hair—what is left of it—tying my tie, putting on my coat. It was only when I attempted to respond to your friendly reception I discovered I had left my teeth in the train." Churchill didn't mind if people saw him naked. He often walked around his country home Chartwell undressed, and he liked to have conversations from the bathtub. Even his female secretaries got an eyeful. One noted in her diary that during the day's work, "I got the best view of his behind that I have ever had. He stepped out of bed still dictating, and oblivious of his all-too-short bed jacket."

Churchill didn't care what anyone else thought. He never shut up; he was rude; he was undignified. And yet . . . and yet strangely this did not mar his dignity but added to it.

Churchill's greatest fault was the fault of his greatest virtue: he was sufficient for himself. His disdain for others' opinions gave him his own clear vision, and he saw what others missed. Willingness to consider all points of view can be a source of weakness as well as strength; in 1940, Churchill knew the true course and led the way without listening to anyone.

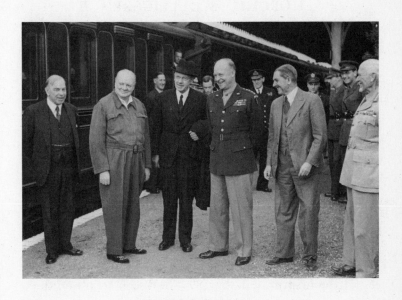

In May 1944, touring with Dominion Prime Ministers to inspect Allied troops participating in the liberation of Europe, Churchill unabashedly wears his siren suit.

13

Churchill's Belligerence

His Defining Characteristic

Virtues and vices—like carpets and hats—obey the law of fashion, and at different times, society, with infuriating inconsistency, punishes or rewards the same trait. What characteristic, in Churchill, won him adulation and honors? The same characteristic that earned him censure: his love of war. He never changed, but the values of the world did.

On his twenty-first birthday, Churchill heard bullets hit bodies for the first time and by 1899, he'd seen action on three continents. When he became Prime Minister in 1940, he'd served in the Army, Navy, and Air Force; been a member of Lloyd George's and Chamberlain's War Cabinets; and got a reputation as someone who couldn't resist a fight.

For good or for ill, right or wrong, Churchill's stomach for war was the defining aspect of his career. While others shrank from battle, Churchill embraced it. War allowed him to channel his belligerency into the flood of something finer, something real, historic. It gave him his greatest moments of adventure and opportunity: the first thrills of battle, his celebrated escape from the Boer camp in 1899, the rigors of the Great War, the stern days of 1940 and 1941. Churchill dismissed those who derided war. "People talked a lot of nonsense when they said wars never settled anything; nothing in history was ever settled except by wars." "Look at the Swiss! They have enjoyed peace for centuries. And what have they produced? The cuckoo clock!" He told Siegfried Sassoon, a poet who wrote about war's horrors, "War is the normal occupation of man" (but then corrected himself, "war—and gardening").

Certainly Churchill was always eager to fight. After leaving Sandhurst in 1896, he strove to push his way into battle, whether as war correspondent or as soldier. He exploited all his parents' connections in high circles—his mother left "no stone unturned, no cutlet uncooked"—to secure a place for him. He was frustrated by the difficulty of getting into action. "Nowadays," he complained in an 1896 letter, "every budding war is spoiled and nipped by some wily diplomatist."

War was no remote exercise for Churchill. He personally killed at close range and, after one battle on horseback, wrote his mother that he "rode up to individuals firing my pistol in their faces and killing several—3 for certain—2 doubtful—one very doubtful." Years later, he chose to serve in the trenches of the Western Front, with their terrible alternations of boredom and terror, their lice, their mud and rot. Even as Prime Minister, Churchill longed to be in action. On D-Day, only the insistence of the King himself stopped Churchill from sailing with the fleet.

To his regret, over his lifetime Churchill saw war deteriorate from a splendid clash of manly combatants to a statistical race of mass production and indiscriminate slaughter—a contest in which a methodical Speer was far more dangerous than a valiant Rommel. Later, recalling the pageantry of the old battles, Churchill wrote, "It is a shame that War should have flung all this aside in its greedy, base, opportunist march, and should turn instead to chemists in spectacles, and chauffeurs pulling the levers of aeroplanes or machine guns."

Churchill didn't hide his frank zest for war. "This, this is living History!" he exulted during World War I. "Everything we are doing and saying is thrilling—it will be read by a thousand generations, think of that! Why, I would not be out of this glorious delicious war for anything the world could give me."

The public was suspicious of his attitude. In 1922, Clementine campaigned for him and reported that voters seemed to object to his enthusiasm for war, but that she was presenting him as a "Cherub Peace Maker" with "fluffy wings round your chubby face." This peacemaker Churchill was unconvincing, and he lost the election. Then, and during the 1930s, and again after World War II, Churchill's eagerness for war cost him public support.

Beneath his happy truculence, however, Churchill recognized the cost of war. He wrote to Clementine in 1909, "Much as war attracts me & fascinates my mind with its tremendous situations—I feel more deeply every year—& can measure the feeling here in the midst of arms—what vile & wicked folly & barbarism it all is."

Churchill's affinity for war sprang in part from his faith in the possibility of a glorious death. As Prime Minister, he inspired people with this conviction that death, if it must come, would be meaningful: life was precious, but not more precious than liberty. Of the desperate months when Britain stood alone, Churchill wrote, "This was a time when it was equally good to live or die." When he visited his former school Harrow during the war, students added to the school song a new verse, in his honor, about the "darker days" of the war. Churchill asked that the word *darker* be changed to *sterner*—because, he said, they were not dark days, they were great days.

Churchill's great wartime command suited him perfectly. His faults were harnessed to his great task, and he surprised everyone with his terrific ability. His natural bellicosity had frequently got him into trouble, but in England's danger, Churchill's fighting nature helped, not hurt, him. He'd worked to prevent the war, but he was also glad to fight; he'd do anything, and suffer anything, before surrendering. He promised the demoralized French in 1940, "Whatever you may do, we shall fight on for ever and ever and ever."

And if the years before 1940 were a prelude, the years after the war were a long decline. In the 1945 election, even before Japan surrendered, Churchill was ejected from office. The public sensed in him the permanent relish for battle, and they wanted no more of it.

Out of office, however, Churchill continued to fight. He criticized the domestic and imperial policies of Labour, and when public sentiment changed, he returned as Prime Minister in 1951. But this time, instead of issues of war and peace, he faced economic problems. In wartime, the country was united behind a single goal, *victory,* and behind a single man, *Churchill;* peace brought disagreements about both ends and means. Churchill observed in 1954 that during the war, "We always knew exactly where we stood, and we had the power to act as we thought best. Now everything is different. There is so much patter, patter, patter, chatter, chatter, chatter it's a wonder anything ever gets done."

Nothing was the same after 1945. Churchill once confided to his doctor, "I feel very lonely without a war. Do you feel like that?" During the war, Churchill had made famous use of his ACTION THIS DAY labels, which he stuck on his most urgent orders to ensure immediate action. The staff loyally preserved the labels in case of Churchill's return, and when he again became Prime Minister in 1951, a stack was placed on his desk. But times had changed. The labels stayed there for more than three years and were never used.

Is it a virtue or a fault to thrive on war? "In great or small station, in Cabinet or in the firing line, alive or dead, my policy is, 'Fight on.' " In *The World Crisis,* Churchill observed, "Nations as well as individuals come to ruin through the over-exercise of those very qualities and faculties on which their dominion has been founded." All gifts are not suited to all seasons; Churchill was punished for his combativeness at other times, but it was his aptitude for war that fitted him for his greatest days.

14

Churchill's Time Line

Key Events

As an attempt to mark all the crucial events in Churchill's life, the conventional time line surely fails. His arrival at Harrow rates the same emphasis as the surrender of Germany, and so many milestones are left out: the appearance of his nanny, Woom—his vow to one day become Prime Minister—the day he received his father's cruel letter—his first game of polo—the sleepless night in 1938—his first stroke—the day he painted for the last time. These are not the kinds of events that usually appear on time lines.

WINSTON LEONARD SPENCER CHURCHILL
(1874–1965)

1874
  Born November 30, at Blenheim Palace
1888
  Entered Harrow

1893

Entered Royal Military College at Sandhurst as cavalry cadet

1895

Death of his father

Commissioned in the Fourth Hussars

1895–1898

Military service in India and the Sudan

Publication of *The Story of the Malakand Field Force* (1898)

1899

Stood for and lost his first election

Escaped Boer prisoner-of-war camp

Publication of *The River War*

1900

Elected Conservative Member of Parliament

Publication of *Savrola*

Publication of *London to Ladysmith via Pretoria*

Publication of *Ian Hamilton's March*

1904

Joined Liberal Party

1905–1908

Undersecretary of State for the Colonies

1906

Publication of *Lord Randolph Churchill*

1908

Married Clementine Hozier

Publication of *My African Journey*

1908–1910

President of the Board of Trade

1910–1911

Home Secretary

1911–1915

First Lord of the Admiralty

1915

Failure of the Dardanelles campaign

Chancellor of the Duchy of Lancaster

1915–1916

Lieutenant colonel in France

1917–1919

Minister of Munitions

1919–1921

Secretary of State for War and Air

1921–1922

Colonial Secretary

Death of his mother

1922

Bought Chartwell Manor

1923

Publication of *The World Crisis* (1923–1931)

1924

Rejoined Conservative Party

1924–1929

Chancellor of the Exchequer

1930

Publication of *My Early Life*

1932

Publication of *Thoughts and Adventures*

1933

Publication of *Marlborough: His Life and Times* (1933–1938)

1937

Publication of *Great Contemporaries*

1939–1940

First Lord of the Admiralty

1940–1945

Prime Minister and Minister of Defense

1940

Battle of Britain

1941

First wartime meeting with Roosevelt

Soviet Union and United States enter the war

1944

Allied invasion of Normandy

1945

Surrender of Germany

Defeated in the general election

Surrender of Japan

1945–1951

Leader of the Opposition

Publication of *The Second World War* (1948–1954)

Publication of *Painting as a Pastime* (1948)

1951–1955

Prime Minister

1953

Awarded Nobel Prize in literature

Created Knight of the Garter

1956

Publication of *A History of the English-Speaking Peoples* (1956–1958)

1959

Won his last election to the House of Commons

1963

Made honorary citizen of the United States

1965

Died January 24

15

CHURCHILL AS SON

His Most Formative Role

Cut off from any unrecorded thought or gesture, biographers can't divine what drives their subjects: they must guess or accept their subjects' claims.

Churchill always insisted that his greatest influence was his father. He memorized his father's words, wrote his biography, imitated his career, and shared his qualities of wit, extravagance, arrogance, ambition, and love for drink and gambling. From his childhood until his death, Churchill longed to be close to his father.

"The greatest and most powerful influence in my early life," Winston Churchill explained, "was of course my father. Although I had talked with him so seldom and never for a moment on equal terms, I conceived an intense admiration and affection for him; and, after his early death, for his memory." In fact, Winston Churchill had two fathers. One was the cold, disapproving father who died when Winston was twenty; the other was the father whom Winston invented after the real one died.

Lord Randolph's political career was packed into a few years and crowned by his appointment as Chancellor of the Exchequer in 1886, at the astonishingly young age of thirty-seven. Winston, then eleven, was immensely proud of his father and kept a scrapbook of news stories and cartoons. He imitated his father in every way he could, even, while at Harrow, asking for a bulldog, just like his father had had at Eton.

Randolph was a brilliant politician; he was also famously arrogant and rude. A family friend recalled that once, when Randolph was cornered by a bore, he summoned a waiter and said, "Waiter—please listen to the end of Colonel B's story."

Randolph's overconfidence led to his political suicide within months of reaching high office. In December 1886, he submitted a budget; the Prime Minister rejected it; to force the issue, Randolph submitted his resignation; and the Prime Minister calmly allowed him to resign. With that miscalculated risk, Randolph's career crashed to an end. Only nine years later, at age forty-five, he died, after a long, degenerative illness marked by a savage temper, increasingly bizarre behavior, and physical breakdown. Though questioned by recent studies, syphilis has commonly been given as the cause of death. The day of Randolph's death—January 24, 1895—was seventy years to the day before his son was to die.

Randolph did little to earn his son's adulation. He scorned

Winston's hero worship and efforts at intimacy; once, he suggested that Winston substitute "Father" for "Papa" in his letters. Randolph rarely spoke or wrote to Winston, except to criticize and to make dire predictions—many of which his son would later fulfill, strikingly, in precise opposite. Randolph once returned one of Winston's letters with a note: "This is a letter which I shall not keep but return to you that you may from time to time review its pedantic & overgrown schoolboy style." In July 1893, eighteen-year-old Winston took the Sandhurst examination for the third time. To his great relief, he managed to qualify for the cavalry, though he missed the necessary score for the infantry. Winston's reaction was to see the benefits of this result: "What fun it would be having a horse! Also the uniforms of the cavalry were far more magnificent than those of the Foot." His father's response was to write a brutal letter:

[In failing to qualify for the infantry] is demonstrated beyond refutation your slovenly happy-go-lucky harum scarum style of work. . . . I am certain that if you cannot prevent yourself from leading the idle useless unprofitable life you have had during your schooldays & later months, you will become a mere social wastrel . . . and you will degenerate into a shabby unhappy & futile existence.

Even Winston, with his tremendous loyalty, admitted that the severe letter startled him.

Winston wanted to learn politics from Randolph, but they had only a few serious conversations. "He seemed to own the key to everything or almost everything worth having," Winston wrote. "But if ever I began to show the slightest idea of comradeship, he was immediately offended; and when once I suggested that I might help his private secretary to write some of his letters, he froze me into stone." When his father died, Winston recalled, "All my dreams of comradeship with him, of entering Parliament at his side and in his support, were ended. There remained for me only to pursue his aims and vindicate his memory."

After Randolph died, however, Winston could replace a critical living father with a noble, inspiring dead father. Alive, Randolph would have continued to accuse him of "incessant complaints and total want of application." In *My Early Life,* Winston joked about his father's low opinion of him, but he didn't deny it. He described the day his father came to see his toy soldiers in battle formation:

> He spent twenty minutes studying the scene. . . . At the end he asked me if I would like to go into the Army. I thought it would be splendid to command an Army, so I said "Yes" at once. . . . For years I thought my father with his experience and flair had discerned in me the qualities of military genius. But I was told later that he had only come to the conclusion that I was not clever enough to go to the Bar.

This was the opinion of the living father. With that father safely dead, Winston reinvented him. He memorized huge portions of his father's speeches. He wrote a two-volume biography, *Lord Randolph Churchill,* that valorized his father's political career. Winston concluded his maiden speech in the House of Commons with an allusion to his father: "I cannot sit down without saying how very grateful I am for the kindness and patience with which the House has heard me, and which have been extended to me, I well know, not on my own account, but because of a certain splendid memory which many honourable Members still preserve."

Winston's devotion to that "certain splendid memory" was devotion to an idol, not his real father. His version of Randolph was unrecognizable. No one disputed that Randolph had been brilliant and effective; he'd also been haughty, opinionated, and unstable. His mottled reputation hung over Winston, especially early on, when many of Randolph's contemporaries remained in power. Winston exploited his father's high connections, but he also suffered from Randolph's notoriety as an adventurer, opportunist, and gadfly (the same labels were applied to Winston). Some predicted that with his rash, thoughtless nature, Winston would self-destruct as his father had done.

Was the driving force of Winston's ambition his compulsion to prove himself to his ever-absent father? In 1924, when Prime Minister Baldwin named Winston as Chancellor of the Exchequer, he said, "This fulfils my ambition. I still have my father's robes as Chancellor." Winston followed— and surpassed—his father's accomplishments. But of course, the dead Randolph could never be confronted with these triumphs. In 1947, during a family dinner, Winston's daughter Sarah asked, "If you had the power to put someone in that chair to join us now, whom would you choose?" His children expected him to pick Julius Caesar or Napoleon. He replied, "Oh, my father, of course." At the end of his life, he decided to be buried not at his beloved country house, Chartwell, but in the churchyard near Blenheim Palace, to be with his father.

Beneath Winston's tremendous stature as a world leader, his belligerence, his confidence, there ran this dark, poignant thread, of a son working vainly to win his father's approval.

Lord Randolph Churchill,
a few years before his death.

16

CHURCHILL AS FATHER

A Good Parent?

Winston Churchill Was a Good Parent

Churchill was a loving father and as attentive as his crowded life permitted. Throughout his life, his letters show a close involvement in his family's activities and health.

When his children were young, he loved to play charades, build sand castles, and chase them in games of "gorilla." He often read to his children before bedtime, from books like *Treasure Island* or Kipling's stories. When they were older, father and children spent happy hours working on Chartwell construction projects, and his children were allowed to join in adult meals and to mingle with the important guests who visited. Later, the war strengthened their bonds, because Churchill took a lively interest in his children's war work.

With his affectionate heart, Churchill felt deeply the death of his daughter Marigold, who died of meningitis before her third birthday. Months later, he wrote Clementine, "I pass through again those sad scenes of last year when we lost our dear duckadilly. Poor lamb—it is a gaping wound, whenever one touches it & removes the bandages & plasters of daily life."

In childhood and as adults, Churchill's children followed his political career with pride, and each encouraged and supported him. When a friend criticized Churchill's war memoirs, Sarah reassured her father, "You are the best historian, the best journalist, the best poet. . . . [W]rite this book from the heart of yourself, from the knowledge you have, and let it stand or fall by that. It will stand." Randolph, Sarah, and Mary wrote admiring books about their father.

Winston Churchill Was Not a Good Parent

Churchill's children suffered from his frequent absences, his disruptive presence, and the tremendous pressure of having a world figure as a father. He was often away from home, not only for official business but also for vacations, where he made his own plans away from the uproar of his large family. For example, barely two weeks after the death of his two-year-old daughter Marigold, Churchill left to visit the Duke of Sutherland. Only months later, Churchill traveled to France while Clementine stayed home with a house full of children and servants suffering from influenza. Clementine collapsed from nervous exhaustion; Churchill stayed in France.

Churchill enjoyed his children in the brief moments he spared for them, but he left the burden of raising and disciplining them to Clementine. Her task was made much harder by Churchill's indulgence—particularly of Randolph, whom Churchill spoiled terribly. Also, Churchill's personal and public demands on Clementine were so great that she didn't spend much time with the children, either. "We soon became aware," their daughter Mary recalled, "that our parents' main interest and time were consumed by immensely important tasks, besides which our own demands and concerns were trivial."

As adults, most of Churchill's children were unhappy and unsuccessful. Arguments and scandal caused constant friction within the family, and alcoholism, depression, bad marriages, and the craving for fame without the talent to win it clouded their lives, except the youngest, Mary.

Randolph, in particular, had a stunted and angry existence. Winston tried to cure the disdain he'd felt from his own father by lavishing attention on his son. Accustomed to indulgence and deference from Winston, as an adult Randolph became overbearing when success didn't come easily. Churchill himself lamented that his son had "great guns but no ammunition." Randolph had some of his father's abilities, loaded with all his father's faults and bad habits, much aggravated. Winston made cutting remarks in the House of Commons; Randolph bellowed at his wife in a restaurant. Winston smoked and drank but was far outpaced by Randolph, who each day smoked eighty to a hundred cigarettes and drank two bottles of whiskey.

Randolph's bad qualities made him very unpopular; despite many tries, and his obvious advantages, he never won a

contested election as MP. As he grew older, and his belligerence strained his relationship with his father, he saw himself
cruelly shoved aside in Churchill's affections by surrogate
sons: Brendan Bracken, who did nothing to discourage rumors that he was Winston's illegitimate son, and Randolph's
brothers-in-law Duncan Sandys and particularly Christopher
Soames, who were influential politicians and intimate advisers to his father, as Randolph wanted to be.

17

CHURCHILL THE PAINTER

His Favorite Pastime

A natural subject of curiosity about a great figure like Churchill is his use of leisure. Churchill had many hobbies, but his favorite pastime was oil painting. His love for painting poses a contradiction: on the one hand, it shows he wasn't content to excel in politics and writing but pushed to extend himself in a secondary talent; on the other hand, it shows that, ambitious as he was, Churchill found time to paint, to occupy himself with color and form, though irrelevant to his worldly position.

Churchill's tremendous energies weren't exhausted by politics and writing, and he enjoyed a hodgepodge of pastimes as well. "To be really happy and really safe," Churchill believed, "one ought to have at least two or three hobbies." He was a firm believer in recreation, especially for those with heavy responsibilities:

Many remedies are suggested for the avoidance of worry and mental overstrain. . . . Some advise exercise, and others,

Churchill painted only one picture during World War II,
of Marrakech, which he considered "the most lovely spot in the world."
He later gave The Tower of Katoubia Mosque
(1943) to President Roosevelt.

repose. Some counsel travel, and others, retreat. Some praise solitude, and others, gaiety. . . . But the element which is constant and common in all of them is Change. . . . A man can wear out a particular part of his mind by continually using it and tiring it, just in the same way as he can wear out the elbows of his coat.

Some leaders lack the intensity that makes a relaxing hobby necessary, but for those who need it, a pastime provides relief. Churchill's own activities demonstrate the astonishing range of his character: bricklaying, landscaping, butterfly collecting, horse racing, keeping tropical fish, feeding swans, hunting, and playing polo. What he loved most, however, was painting.

Restless, gregarious, verbose, he found relief in the solitude and color of his canvas. Churchill discovered painting in the summer of 1915, one of the lowest periods of his life. As First Lord of the Admiralty, he championed the Dardanelles campaign, and its failure led to his shattering expulsion from office. His conviction that his plan could have brought an important victory, and the impotence of watching from the sidelines, drove Churchill to near despair. "In this position I knew everything and could do nothing," he recalled. "Like a sea-beast fished up from the depths, or a diver too suddenly hoisted, my veins threatened to burst from the fall in pressure."

Solace came unexpectedly. One Sunday morning in the country, Churchill became fascinated with experiments with a child's paint box; four days later, he was completely outfitted for painting in oil. Confronted with a white canvas and gleaming palette, however, even Churchill was daunted. He hesitated, and just then, his neighbor, a painter, drove by. She stopped, slashed Churchill's pristine canvas with some strokes of blue, and drove away his inhibitions. From then on, from his fortieth until his eighty-fifth year, when in the south of

France he set up his easel for the last time, Churchill painted when he could. Despite his sound advice about the importance of relaxation, however, even Churchill didn't have the time to paint during the frantic days of World War II. He painted only one picture, in Marrakech, which he gave to Roosevelt. (After one illness, Churchill announced that he was strong enough to fight Germans but still too weak to paint a picture.)

He was proud of his painterly ability, and even in this area drove to excel. "Every ambition I've ever had has been fulfilled—save one," he once admitted. "I am not a *great* painter." In 1947, he submitted two paintings to the Royal Academy under a pseudonym. Of the hundreds of pictures considered, the judges included his among the few to hang in the annual exhibition.

Churchill loved his own pictures—in fact, he almost never gave one away—but he was indifferent to art and didn't visit galleries or museums. He was only interested in capturing his own impressions and basking in others' admiration of his work.

Why did oil paints and canvas appeal so deeply to Churchill? Perhaps because painting gave him an escape from everything that tired him about himself. Churchill was an indefatigable talker and, even as a writer, worked with a large team of typists, researchers, and aides. Painting gave him relief from his own relentless nature: only while painting could he remain silent for long. Few people appear in his paintings. Most of them are sunny landscapes, light on water, Chartwell scenes, or still-life interiors.

His painting took him out of the gloom of the House of Commons and the antagonisms of public life, into the bright light of nature. It was a relief to turn his attention to the serene problems of shade and color; as he once wrote, "the horrors of war cannot rob the progress of the sun." He loved bright colors ("I rejoice with the brilliant ones, and am genuinely sorry for the poor browns") and sunshine ("Now I am learning to like painting even on dull days. But in my hot youth I demanded sunshine"). It was sunshine that drew him so often to France, the foreign country that he visited far more often than any other. And although in life he was witness to enormous changes in technology, weaponry, and society, in painting he could sink into timeless views.

He found a deep sensual pleasure in painting: "The colours are lovely to look at and delicious to squeeze out. Matching them, however crudely, with what you see is fascinating and absolutely absorbing." A painter who helped Churchill with his technique remarked of Churchill that "[h]e would have eaten a tube of white he loved the smell of it so."

Painting came to his rescue after the shock of the Dardanelles disaster in 1915. Painting was also his great consolation after the ordeal of 1945, when Churchill lost the Prime Ministership in the midst of triumph. Several weeks after the Labour victory, he and his daughter Sarah traveled to Italy. After years of grueling work, constant meetings, and endless red dispatch boxes, Churchill spent his days of enforced leisure in painting and picnicking; the hours in front of the canvas restored some measure of peace after the blow of the election.

"Happy are the painters," wrote Churchill, "for they shall not be lonely. Light and colour, peace and hope, will keep them company to the end, or almost to the end, of the day."

18

CHURCHILL THE SPENDTHRIFT

A Weakness

Money dictates the circumstances of a subject's life, and no biography can ignore it. Churchill, it happens, was habitually careless with money. This unattractive fact about Churchill shouldn't be neglected, however, because it sheds light on other important aspects of his personality: his disdain for other people's opinions, his massive productivity, his expectation that his needs be met, his demand for beauty and comfort.

One of Churchill's most obvious qualities was his self-absorption, and one of the most obvious manifestations of this quality was his persistent trouble with money. Churchill was one of those heedless people who never thinks much about expenses and trusts that any difficulties will remedy themselves. He had a clear view of what his standard of living should be, and he spent as he needed, not as he had.

In this, he was like his spendthrift father and mother: he

exhibited the worst habits of careless British aristocrats and American nouveaux riches. Randolph and Jennie indulged in extravagances they couldn't afford, and their son followed their example. It is the privilege of the aristocrat to ignore his bills. Six years after joining the Fourth Hussars, Churchill was still stalling the tailor who made his first uniforms. He ignored stacks of bills for wine, books, equipment. With lordly disdain for shopkeepers, he wrote his mother in 1897, "If I had not been so foolish as to pay a lot of bills I should have the money now."

Churchill always managed to live well—"throughout his life the bells he rang were always answered"—but because his parents spent most of their money on themselves, he had to earn his own way. He didn't, however, resort to the solution, then popular with impoverished British aristocrats, of marrying an heiress. Although descended from one of Scotland's great families, Clementine had grown up in genteel poverty.

While becoming the head of a family often has a steadying effect, it didn't change Churchill. His carelessness was an unceasing irritation for the frugal, nervous Clementine. In the early days of their marriage, for example, she was shocked by how much he spent on underclothes—finely woven silk of pale pink, required, he claimed, by his sensitive skin.

Despite their financial straits, Churchill refused to scrimp. His periodic attempts to impose a family budget didn't help, because it was *he* who wouldn't economize. He dismissed his wife's anxieties with the nonchalance of one who perpetually disregards the trouble he causes. He wrote to Clementine in September 1928:

> [D]o not worry about household matters. Let them crash if they will. All will be well. Servants exist to save one trouble, & shd never be allowed to disturb ones inner peace. There will always be food to eat, & sleep will come even if the beds are not made. Nothing is worse than worrying about trifles.

This, from a man who didn't tie his own shoelaces or dry himself after his bath but instead depended on his valet; who often lost money gambling; who spent freely on travel, liquor, paint, and his country house; who expected to entertain several times a week; who only once in his life would take the Underground. It seems unlikely his letter had the intended soothing effect.

Though profligate, Churchill did manage to support himself and his family. "I have always had to earn every penny I possessed but there has never been a day in my life when I could not order a bottle of champagne for myself and offer another to a friend." How? By writing. He earned a huge amount for his work and, furthermore, didn't shrink from exploiting his famous name. In the particularly lean period of the 1930s, he was driven to writing for popular magazines on unserious topics such as "The American Mind and Ours," "Iced Water," and "Is There Life on the Moon?" He was paid more than £300 an article to retell famous stories, such as *Anna Karenina* and *Uncle Tom's Cabin,* which, given that he paid an aide only £25 to write the pieces, earned him a tidy profit.

Churchill was able to earn. The problem was that while he earned a fortune writing, he spent a still larger fortune. The family's finances took a blow when Churchill bought the country house Chartwell in 1922. Churchill loved Chartwell, but for Clementine (whom he hadn't consulted about the purchase), it was an unending source of worry. In addition to the expense of the payroll alone—cook, farm-hand, groom, three gardeners, nanny, nursery maid, odd-jobs man, two housemaids, two kitchen maids, and two pantry maids—Churchill was constantly dreaming up money-consuming projects. Stock-market reverses and gambling losses also took a toll. From youth until after the Second World War, Churchill was almost continually in debt.

In fact, only months before the Munich crisis in 1938, Churchill's money troubles drove him to consider quitting Parliament, a move that would have blocked him from the Prime Ministership in 1940. He even considered selling his beloved Chartwell. In one of the fairy-tale solutions that periodically blessed Churchill—as in 1921, when a relative died in a train crash and left his entire Irish estate, worth more than £50,000, to Churchill—an expatriate South African tycoon bailed him out. Even so, Churchill spent much of the critical prewar period holed up at Chartwell, writing (or rather, dictating) as fast as he could to earn money. After the war, finally, his memoirs' success solved his money problems.

Because Churchill liked to enjoy the finest wines, cigars, and surroundings, with wonderful scenery to paint, he lent his prestige to anyone who had a well-appointed villa, private railcar, or yacht. Churchill also willingly accepted lavish gifts, a habit that today, at least, seems quite inappropriate for a politician. One controversial financier paid to furnish his drawing room; another time, a group of friends pitched in to buy him a car; more than once, he was rescued from financial distress by a wealthy patron.

Churchill required that he get everything he wanted, and as a result, a pressing need for money was one of the shaping forces of his career.

19

CONFLICTING VIEWS OF CHURCHILL

How Others Saw Him

When we judge Churchill, we see his life whole, but his contemporaries judged him without the benefit of hindsight. What did they make of Churchill? Did they respect him, or not? Trust him, or not? Like him, or not? Evidence in the record supports contradictory conclusions.

Churchill himself observed, "One mark of a great man is the power of making lasting impressions upon the people he meets." For better or worse, Churchill certainly did so.

About Churchill, contemporary accounts tell us . . .

That many foresaw his great destiny:

> I feel certain that I shall someday shake hands with you as Prime Minister of England. You possess the two necessary qualifications: genius and plod.
>
> —CAPTAIN PERCY SCOTT, IN 1899

That many expected he had no future in public life:

He is absolutely untrustworthy as was his father before him, and he has got to learn that just as his father had to disappear from politics so must he, or at all events from official life.

—LORD DERBY, IN 1916

That he was much like his father:

He is most tiresome to deal with & will I fear give trouble—as his father did—in any position to which he may be called. The restless energy, uncontrollable desire for notoriety & the lack of moral perception make him an anxiety indeed!

—SIR FRANCIS HOPWOOD, IN 1907

That he didn't measure up to his father:

Grimthorpe, a friend of Lord Randolph Churchill, compared the father and son. "It is just the difference between great capacity and genius. Winston has great ability, but he has not the genius of his father."

—LORD GRIMTHORPE

That even his critics admitted he had great qualities:

First impression: restless—almost intolerably so, without capacity for sustained and unexciting labour—egotistical, bumptious, shallow-minded and reactionary, but with a certain personal magnetism, great pluck and some originality—not of intellect, but of character.

—BEATRICE WEBB, IN 1903

That even his admirers admitted he had many limitations:

He has the defects of his qualities, and as his qualities are large, the shadow which they throw is fairly large also; but I say deliberately, in my judgment, in mental power and vital force he is one of the foremost men in our country.

—ANDREW BONAR LAW, IN 1915

That he was a gifted strategist:

So far every step he contemplates is good, *and he is brave, which is everything! Napoleonic in audacity, Cromwellian in thoroughness.*

—LORD FISHER, IN 1912

That he was a poor strategist:

A complete amateur of strategy, he swamps himself in details he should never look at and as a result fails ever to see a strategic problem in its true perspective.

—GENERAL SIR ALAN BROOKE, IN 1944

That he could captivate a crowd with his eloquence:

To listen to him on the platform or in the House is sheer delight. The art of arrangement, the unexpected turn, the flashes
of sparkling humour, and the torrent of picturesque adjectives
combine to put his speeches in a class by themselves.

—NEVILLE CHAMBERLAIN, IN 1928

That he could weary a dinner party with his monologues:

For nearly four hours a figure out of history had talked to
us without reserve, and yet those who heard him appeared
half asleep.

—LORD MORAN, IN 1945

That he was admired by those who served under him:

The man's as brave as six, as good-humored, shrewd, self-
confident & considerate as a statesman can be: & several
times I've seen him chuck the statesmanlike course & do
the honest thing instead.

—T. E. LAWRENCE, IN 1921

That he was disliked by those who served under him:

One of the men in your entourage (a devoted friend) has
been to me & told me that there is a danger of your being

generally disliked by your colleagues and subordinates because of your rough sarcastic & overbearing manner . . .
you are supposed to be so contemptuous that presently no
ideas, good or bad, will be forthcoming.

—CLEMENTINE CHURCHILL, IN 1940

That he showed tremendous powers of oratory:

I have heard Mr. Churchill in the House of Commons at
intervals over the last ten years. . . . To-day, he was different. There was little oratory; he wasn't interested in being
a showman. He spoke the language of Shakespeare with a
direct urgency such as I have never before heard in that
House. There were no frills and no tricks.

—EDWARD R. MURROW, OF THE JUNE 4, 1940,
"WE SHALL FIGHT ON THE BEACHES" SPEECH

That he sometimes failed to harness his powers of oratory:

How I wish Winston would not talk on the wireless unless he is feeling in good form. He hates the microphone,
and when we bullied him into speaking last night, he just
sulked and read his House of Commons speech over
again. Now, as delivered in the House of Commons, that
speech was magnificent, especially the concluding sentences. But it sounded ghastly on the wireless.

—HAROLD NICOLSON, OF THE JUNE 18, 1940,
"THIS WAS THEIR FINEST HOUR" SPEECH

That he had a deep understanding of the British people:

By dramatising their lives and making them seem to themselves and to each other clad in the fabulous garments appropriate to a great historic moment, [he] transformed cowards into brave men.

—ISAIAH BERLIN

That he had little affinity for ordinary men and women:

His background (combined with the British caste system) made him a person who expected to be approached with great respect by those who worked for him. He was careful to keep each stratum in its proper place.

—ELIZABETH NEL

That he was a great representative of the nation in war:

Winston embodied the soul of the nation. He succeeded in being the nation, for that is what he was. In the simplified conditions of war he could be that, whereas in the more complex days of peace he never was, never could be, that.

—OLIVER FRANKS, IN 1957

That he sought personal gain in war:

When the war came he saw in it the chance of glory for himself, & has accordingly entered on a risky campaign without caring a straw for the misery and hardship it would bring to thousands, in the hope that he would prove to be the outstanding man in this war.

—DAVID LLOYD GEORGE, IN 1915

20

CHURCHILL IN TEARS

Telling Detail

According to Plutarch, in writing lives, "a slight thing like a phrase or a jest often makes a greater revelation of character than battles where thousands fall." Telling details can be deceptive, because they tell whatever the biographer wants them to tell—and yet we crave them. Churchill, surprisingly, often wept. Tears seem out of character with his bulldog nature, but it can be the aspects that seem most uncharacteristic that offer the greatest insights.

Of the many deprecating adjectives lobbed at Churchill—*egotistical, belligerent, stubborn, self-advertising*—one of the most striking is *sentimental*. It's plain why Churchill was accused of this. His rhetoric was often overblown and appealed to capitalized notions of Patriotism and Freedom. He was an indulgent, emotional friend and father. And most oddly—for an adult, a statesman, and an Englishman, given the English emphasis on imperturbability, understatement, and dislike of being conspicuous—he often dissolved in tears. But was he really "sentimental"?

Sentimentality, or exaggerated tears, arises when an emotional reaction exceeds its cause. Churchill comprehended the world with tremendous scope and scale, and his emotions were pitched to match.

He didn't try to hide his tears. "I blub an awful lot, you know," he confessed cheerfully to his new private secretary. "You'll have to get used to it." Everyone noticed it. "Then Lloyd George gets up and makes a moving speech telling Winston how fond he is of him. Winston cries slightly and mops his eyes." "The grand finale ends in an ovation, with Winston sitting there with the tears pouring down his cheeks." "We had two lovely films after dinner. . . . Winston managed to cry through all of them, including the comedy." "Churchill was affected emotionally, as I knew he would be. His handkerchief stole from its pocket." "[H]e quotes Kipling's lines about the mine-sweepers, and is so moved by them that he chokes and cannot continue." "We then find him adopting the attitude that he was the only one trying to win the war, that he was the only one who produced any ideas . . . he worked himself up into such a state from the woeful picture he had painted, that tears streamed down his face!" "Not for one moment did Winston stop crying . . . he could have filled buckets by the time he received the Freedom of Paris."

Another man might have felt these emotions but hidden his tears. Not Churchill. He hid nothing—certainly not for dignity's sake. His peculiar sincerity, and his indifference to other people's opinions, made it hard for him to conceal anything. There he was, Churchill, perfectly obvious. His courage, his manliness, his nerves were beyond question, and he felt no need to hide what he felt. Indeed, far from hiding his tears, Churchill recognized their value. Very early in his life, before he first entered Parliament, he wrote shrewdly, "Before [a speaker] can inspire [an audience] with any emotion he must be swayed by it himself. . . . Before he can move their tears his own must flow."

It's notable that Churchill cried so visibly, but what's more surprising is that he cried at all: adult Englishmen did not often weep. Churchill's strenuous historical vision allowed him to feel passionately the pathos and grandeur of his times. It was the thought of sacrifice or courage that moved him most, as when he visited a very poor London neighborhood that had been devastated by the Blitz:

Already little pathetic Union Jacks had been stuck up amid the ruins. When my car was recognised the people came running from all quarters, and a crowd of more than a thousand was soon gathered. All these folk were in a high state of enthusiasm. They crowded round us, cheering and manifesting every sign of lively affection, wanting to touch and stroke my clothes. One would have thought I had brought them some fine substantial benefit which would improve their lot in life. I was completely undermined, and wept. Ismay, who was with me, records that he heard an old woman say: "You see, he really cares. He's crying." They were tears not of sorrow but of wonder and admiration.

Churchill didn't hesitate to express his emotions in frank, even childish terms—such as his way of referring to Hitler as "that Bad Man." In August 1940, Churchill visited the nerve center of the air battle over Britain, where young pilots were ready to fight and die at a moment's readiness. Churchill's colleague Ismay described the scene: "There had been heavy fighting throughout the afternoon; and at one moment every single squadron in the Group was engaged; there was nothing in reserve, and the map table showed new waves of attackers crossing the coast. I felt sick with fear." After tremendous struggle the Royal Air Force repelled the attack. Later, as the two men sped away to Chequers, Churchill said to Ismay, "Don't speak to me; I have never been so moved." It's hard to imagine another statesman sending the plaintive cable he sent to Roosevelt on April 12, 1942, to confide that a serious disagreement "would break my heart." In March 1945, after telling the House of Commons that David Lloyd George had died, Churchill said, "I do not think we can do any more business today. I feel that should be the feeling of the House."

With his family, his emotions gushed even more. In 1909, he wrote to Clementine, whom he called Cat, Pussy-Cat, or Kat (she called him Mr. Pug or Pig, and he often decorated his letters with drawings of pigs), "Sweet cat—I kiss your vision as it rises before my mind. Your dear heart throbs often in my own. God bless you darling keep you safe & sound. Kiss the P.K. [Puppy Kitten] for me all over. With fondest love—W."

Churchill is identified with many things—his cigars, his V signs, his hats, his love for liquor, his fighting spirit. These emphasize the brave, optimistic side of his character. But Churchill, who promised, "I have nothing to offer but blood, toil, tears and sweat," was unfraid to be seen in tears.

21

CHURCHILL THE DRINKER

An Alcoholic?

Winston Churchill Was an Alcoholic

Churchill drank all day long, every day. He'd have his first whisky and soda—his signature drink—soon after breakfast and kept drinking until he went to sleep. Liquor of several sorts flowed at lunch and dinner.

Churchill's heavy drinking was no secret. When he became Prime Minister, President Roosevelt commented that he "supposed Churchill was the best man that England had, even if he was drunk half of his time." Churchill was recorded to have had eleven whiskies and soda during a single meal. In the space of two weeks, soon after his 1945 ouster, Churchill with only a bit of help consumed ninety-six bottles of champagne while also drinking six or seven whiskies and soda and three brandies each day as well.

Churchill's associates worried about his prodigious consumption, which Churchill did nothing to hide. Offered tea one morning, Churchill asked instead for a glass of white wine. "A tumbler was brought which he drained in one go, and then licked his lips . . . and said, 'Ah! That is good, but you know, I have already had two whiskies and soda and 2 cigars this morning.'!! It was then only shortly after 7:30 A.M." Alan Brooke complained in his diary about alcohol's effect on Churchill: "We had to consider this morning at the [Chiefs of Staff meeting] one of Winston's worst minutes I have ever seen . . . he must have been quite tight when he dictated it."

Churchill made sure never to be far from alcohol. With the Grenadier Guards during World War I, he moved to a company in the line partly to escape the "dry" battalion headquarters. Traveling in the United States during Prohibition, while recovering from having been hit by a car, he procured a doctor's note: "This is to certify that the post-accident convalescence of the Hon. Winston S. Churchill necessitates the use of alcoholic spirits especially at meal times."

This behavior certainly demonstrates a marked and unhealthy dependence on alcohol.

Winston Churchill Was Not an Alcoholic

It's undeniable that Churchill enjoyed liquor and that his consumption, especially by today's far more abstemious standards, was substantial. However, much of his relish for drinking was for show.

Churchill exaggerated his enjoyment of whisky and champagne to create one of his most distinctive characteristics—an idiosyncrasy that everyone recognized and smiled over and that helped make people feel closer to him. As one associate observed, "The glass of weak whisky, like the cigars, was more a symbol than anything else, and one glass lasted him for hours." Each drink was weakened by soda and ice, and Churchill's consumption didn't have much effect. "He was never the worse for drink in my experience," wrote Sir Ian Jacob, "and, as far as I could see, he never felt the slightest ill-effects in the morning." His lisp gave his speech a slurred sound, which may have made him sound drunk to those who didn't know his voice.

Churchill also used his love for liquor as a handy subject for his wit. At a meeting with an Arab ruler, Churchill was told that neither smoking nor drinking of alcohol were customary before a Muslim king. Churchill explained through the interpreter, "My rule of life prescribed as an absolute sacred rite smoking cigars and also the drinking of alcohol before, after, and if need be during all meals and in the intervals between them." "When I was younger," he told King George VI in January 1952, "I made it a rule never to take strong drink before lunch. It is now my rule never to do so before breakfast."

Given Churchill's extraordinary accomplishments—both in public office and in private life—and the positions of responsibility he held until he was in his eighties, it's difficult to credit that dependence on alcohol in any way impaired his health or abilities.

22

CHURCHILL IN CONTEXT

Facts at a Glance

Colorless but useful, bare facts help us grasp the whole of Churchill's life by placing him in context. Neatly ordered, seemingly without interpretation or bias, their precision is comforting. We read these facts; we assume these must be ones that matter.

Churchill's Sovereigns

Queen Victoria—1837–1901; Diamond Jubilee, 1897

King Edward VII—1901–1910

King George V—1910–1936

King Edward VIII—abdicated, December 1936

King George VI—1936–1952

Queen Elizabeth II—1952–present (Elizabeth is Victoria's great-great-granddaughter.)

Prime Ministers During Churchill's Political Career

1895   Salisbury

1902   Balfour

1905   Campbell–Bannerman (Churchill: Undersecretary for the Colonies)

1908   Asquith (Churchill: President of the Board of Trade, Home Secretary, First Lord of the Admiralty)

1916   Lloyd George (Churchill: Minister of Munitions, Secretary of State for War and Air, Colonial Secretary)

1922   Bonar Law

1923   Baldwin

1924   MacDonald

1924   Baldwin (Churchill: Chancellor of the Exchequer)

1929   MacDonald

1935   Baldwin

1937   Chamberlain (Churchill: First Lord of the Admiralty)

1940   Churchill

1945   Attlee

1951   Churchill

1955   Eden

1957   Macmillan

1963   Douglas-Home

1964   Wilson

Churchill's Changing Party Alliances

- In 1900, he entered Parliament as a Conservative.
- In 1904, he left the Conservatives over the issue of free trade and joined the Liberal Party.
- In 1924, he rejoined the Conservative Party.

The British Peerage

The British hereditary peerage comprises five descending grades of nobility: duke, marquess, earl, viscount, and baron. Dukes rank significantly above the four lower grades, and only a duke is addressed as "Your Grace" instead of "My Lord."

A peer passes his title and estate to his eldest son, and his other children, who aren't peers, must be content with courtesy titles. For example, the seventh Duke of Marlborough had two sons who survived to adulthood: the elder became the eighth Duke of Marlborough; the younger was "Lord Randolph," but his children didn't inherit a title. Therefore, Winston Churchill, though the grandson of a Duke, was Mr. Winston Churchill, a commoner. He became "Sir Winston Churchill" in 1953, when, after refusing the distinction for many years, he accepted the Order of the Garter in honor of Queen Elizabeth II's coronation.

Churchill's Executive Positions

1905–1908	Colonial Undersecretary
1908–1910	President of the Board of Trade
1910–1911	Home Secretary
1911–1915	First Lord of the Admiralty
1917–1919	Minister of Munitions
1919–1921	Secretary of State for War and Air
1921–1922	Colonial Secretary
1924–1929	Chancellor of the Exchequer
1929–1939	*"Wilderness years"*

1939–1940   First Lord of the Admiralty

1940–1945   Prime Minister

1951–1955   Prime Minister

Churchill Statistics

- Churchill's height: five feet six inches.
- Churchill's hair color: red.
- The period he described as the unhappiest of his life: his school days at Harrow.
- His best subjects at the Royal Military College at Sandhurst: military topography, tactics, fortifications, horse-riding skills.
- Churchill's age when the first Winston Churchill biography was published: thirty-one.
- Number of silver inkstands he received as wedding gifts: seventeen.
- Months it took him to dictate the first volume of his World War I memoir: three.
- Miles separating the coast of England from the coast of France: twenty-one.
- Temperature constantly maintained in Churchill's bedroom: seventy-four degrees Fahrenheit.
- Temperature maintained in Churchill's bath: ninety-eight degrees Fahrenheit.
- Code name for the preparations for Churchill's state funeral: "Hope Not."
- Weight of Churchill papers, in tons: fifteen.
- Number of times Churchill was on the cover of *Time* magazine: eight.

- Number of canvases he painted during his life: nearly five hundred.
- Whom he believed to be the greatest man who'd ever lived: Julius Caesar, "because he was the most magnanimous of all the conquerors."
- His mother's birthplace: 426 Henry Street, Brooklyn, New York.
- His attendance at church: infrequent.
- Subject of the biography he wanted to write but never did: Napoleon.

Churchill's Regiments

Fourth Hussars

Thirty-first Punjabi Infantry

Twenty-first Lancers

South African Light Horse

Oxfordshire Hussars

Oxfordshire Yeomanry

Grenadier Guards

Royal Scots Fusiliers

Oxfordshire Artillery

Churchill's Favorites

- Favorite whisky: Johnnie Walker Red Label.
- Favorite champagne: Pol Roger 1928. (Churchill named a racehorse Pol Roger.)
- Favorite cheese: Stilton.
- Favorite cigar: Romeo y Julieta.

- Favorite movies: *Lady Hamilton* (Churchill saw it seventeen times), Olivier's *Henry V,* Chaplin's *The Great Dictator.*
- Favorite painting site: Marrakech, in Morocco.
- Favorite pets: his French poodles Rufus I and Rufus II, his cats Whiskey and Marmalade, his bird Toby.
- Favorite card games: bezique, gin rummy, Oklahoma.
- Favorite gift to other people: an autographed, leather-bound copy of one of his own books.
- Some favorite music: Gilbert and Sullivan's comic operas; martial airs; Harrow school songs, particularly "Forty Years On"; Noël Coward tunes; "Rule, Britannia"; "Land of Hope and Glory"; "Tipperary."
- Some favorite hymns: "Mine Eyes Have Seen the Glory of the Coming of the Lord," "Fight the Good Fight with All Thy Might," "O God, Our Help in Ages Past."
- Some favorite books: H. Rider Haggard's *King Solomon's Mines* (Churchill read it twelve times as a boy); T. E. Lawrence's *Seven Pillars of Wisdom;* Anthony Trollope's political novels, especially (unsurprisingly, given the title) *The Duke's Children.*
- Favorite English poet: A. E. Housman.
- Author most often quoted: Shakespeare, particularly *King John, Richard III, Hamlet.*
- A favorite aphorism: "*On ne règne sur les âmes que par le calme.*"
- A favorite Bible verse: "Thou shalt not muzzle the ox that treadeth out the corn."

• A favorite wartime poem: Arthur Hugh Clough's "Say Not the Struggle Nought Availeth."

> For while the tired waves, vainly breaking,
> Seem here no painful inch to gain,
> Far back through creeks and inlets making
> Came silent, flooding in, the main,
>
> And not by eastern windows only,
> When daylight comes, comes in the light,
> In front the sun climbs slow, how slowly,
> But westward, look, the land is bright.

Notes on the British Form of Government, in Comparison to That of the United States

The British Parliament is divided into two Houses: the House of Lords, made up of peers, and the House of Commons, made up of elected representatives. Members of the House of Commons are elected at a general election; if a Member of Parliament (MP) dies or retires between elections, the constituency elects a new MP at a by-election. Unlike the United States, where a candidate must live in a place to represent it, a candidate need not have lived in the constituency to "stand" for election there.

The British system doesn't follow a rigid schedule of elections. A parliament may (but often doesn't) last as long as five years; it also has the power to extend itself. For example, rather than hold a general election in wartime, the parliaments elected in 1910 and 1935 prolonged their lives, year by year, until 1918 and 1945, respectively. Thus, for example, Harold Nicolson was an MP—after winning a slender majority in a single election—for ten crucial years, from 1935 to 1945.

In the United States, the executive and the legislative branches are distinct. The U.S. President is elected separately from the members of Congress, and he chooses whomever he wants to serve in his cabinet (subject to Senate confirmation).

In Britain, the executive and the legislative functions are intertwined. The British Prime Minister is not elected as such but generally takes that office as one who commands a majority in the House of Commons (usually, but not necessarily, the Prime Minister is head of the majority party); the Prime Minister appoints ministers who are, with virtually no exception, drawn from the House of Commons or the House of Lords (as if, in the United States, the President could appoint only Representatives and Senators to cabinet positions). This circumstance makes individual ministers more independent from the Prime Minister than American cabinet members are from the President.

Subject to Senate confirmation, a U.S. President has the power to appoint not only cabinet secretaries but also a huge number of their deputies, assistants, and other officials. By contrast, a Prime Minister appoints only the heads of the different branches. Ministers are intended to set broad policy outlines and leave the actual administration of their departments to the permanent civil service.

23

CHURCHILL AND SEX

Too Interesting to Ignore

Biographers often justify their prying into a subject's intimate life by making more or less plausible leaps from private to public: Jefferson's conduct influenced his attitude toward slavery; Picasso's lovers inspired his art; a philandering politican may cheat the public; a closet homosexual may have more to hide.

But we don't need to justify our curiosity with the unconvincing fig leaf of public relevance. If the goal is to understand a subject's character, sexual life is too interesting to ignore.

In many cases, the facts about a subject's intimate life confound our expectations. We expect personalities to be unified, but sex often proves how unpredictable people can be. In Churchill's case—given his high energy, his urge to dominate, his attraction to luxury and beauty, and his disdain for other people's opinions—perhaps the surprise is the apparent decorousness of his intimate life.

Along with Karl Marx, the greatest contemporary intellectual influence of Churchill's era was Sigmund Freud.

Although the Freudian revolution—with its emphasis on how sexuality determines character—seems to have had little effect on how Churchill viewed the world, Freud changed how the world views Churchill. A modern biography must examine the issue of Churchill and sex.

Churchill didn't show much interest in sex.

Often great leaders are flirtatious and promiscuous; they touch and hug, seduce and abandon. Their predatory sexuality charges their charisma.

Churchill lacked this quality. He was sufficient for himself and indifferent to sexual distractions. Unmoved by the flirtatious banter of a dinner party or the heady seduction of a crowd, he sought the company of men and was happiest in an atmosphere of cigars, port, newspapers, and political talk. A close friend described him as without "strong sexual desires." Churchill himself reportedly joked that "the reason I can write so much is that I don't waste my essence in bed."

Historians William Manchester and A.J.P. Taylor maintain that Churchill was "undersexed" and hypothesize that his mother's promiscuity stunted his sexual development. This seems a bit rough on Jennie; while she certainly had many affairs, as was common in her set, Churchill doesn't seem to have been particularly disturbed by that fact. The belief or suspicion that syphilis caused his father's humiliating, wasting death at age forty-five seems a more likely explanation. In any case, whether Churchill was in fact "undersexed" is disputable; after all, Churchill and Clementine were married less than a month after announcing their engagement, and Clementine was pregnant within a month of their wedding, or even before, and she became pregnant six times (one pregnancy ended in miscarriage).

Over the course of Churchill's long life in the public eye, almost inevitably a few rumors of sexual impropriety swirled around him. Most improbable was the charge, in 1895, that he was guilty of "acts of gross immorality of the Oscar Wilde type." These accusations were withdrawn, and his accuser apologized. He was also rumored to have fathered illegitimate children. Brendan Bracken, one of Churchill's most loyal supporters, encouraged the rumor that he was Churchill's son, and because of Churchill's fondness for that somewhat limited man, many people believed it. However, there's no evidence that Churchill had an illegitimate child.

Citing only "personal information," Manchester hints darkly at a single act of infidelity, sometime before 1932, "with a divorced, titled Englishwoman whose seductive skills and sexual experience far exceeded his." Also, in his last years, Churchill frequently visited Emery Reves and Wendy Russell at their luxurious French villa, and some observers—including Clementine—were uncomfortable with the affection between Churchill and his hostess. Noël Coward bitingly described Churchill as "absolutely obsessed with a senile passion for Wendy Russell. He followed her about the room with his brimming eyes and wobbled after her across the terrace, staggering like a vast baby of two who is just learning to walk." But these episodes stand as exceptions. Churchill was a faithful husband.

Churchill's writings reflect his lack of interest in sex and its influence. Although he was fascinated by personality, his

Victorian-style biographies and character sketches don't speculate in modern fashion about their subjects' sexual drives.

If he chose, Churchill certainly had occasion to comment on the carnal influences on public figures. For example, he forbore to mention Prime Minister Asquith's passionate— and politically indiscreet—relationship with Venetia Stanley, even though this relationship had had serious consequences for Churchill. While Churchill's Dardanelles campaign was being executed, the sixty-two-year-old Prime Minister was writing love letters during Cabinet meetings to twenty-seven-year-old Venetia. When, in May 1915, Asquith learned that his soul mate had become engaged to another man, his anguish distracted him from public affairs at a moment of political crisis; otherwise, he might have been able to save his government. Instead, he formed a coalition government—and a condition of the coalition, imposed by the Conservatives, was Churchill's removal at a time when his great campaign, and his reputation, were at stake. Nor did fascination with T. E. "Lawrence of Arabia," with his flowing robes, charisma, and abandonment of powerful position to become an ordinary soldier under assumed names, induce Churchill to speculate about the dark desires haunting (quite obviously) Lawrence's extraordinary personality. In *Marlborough,* Churchill did expand on the romantic passion between John Churchill and his wife, Sarah, and on Princess, later Queen, Anne's "strangely intense affection" for Sarah. Even here, however, Churchill accepted appearances and didn't probe for hidden impulses.

Churchill took his sport not from flirtation or dissipation but from wall building, lake digging, and painting. He was preoccupied with military and political battles, with the known lives of great figures and the development of historic institutions. His pleasures, and his anguish, came from grand public dramas rather than from intimate episodes.

24

CHURCHILL AS HUSBAND

A Happy Marriage?

Winston Churchill Had a Happy Marriage

Winston and Clementine met in April 1908, and in September, they married; he was thirty-three years old, she, ten years younger. They had five children and were married for more than fifty years.

Although they had very different temperaments, they were devoted to each other. Consider this pair of letters, exchanged in March 1916, while Winston was at the front in France during World War I. Clementine wrote of her hope that at their next meeting they would find time to spend alone, before their love had been replaced by "friendship"—"peaceful but not very stimulating."

Winston's letters reveal an understanding of himself and his limitations, and his love for Clementine. He wrote back:

Oh my darling do not write of "friendship" to me—I love you more each month that passes and feel the need of you & all your beauty. My precious charming Clemmie—I too feel sometimes the longing for rest & peace. . . .

Sometimes also I think I wd not mind stopping living vy much—I am so devoured by egoism that I wd like to have another soul in another world & meet you in another setting, & pay you all the love and honour of the gt romances.

During a lifetime of exceptional strain and anxiety, they were each other's best comforters and staunchest supports.

Winston Churchill Did Not Have a Happy Marriage

Winston's memoir *My Early Life* ends like a fairy tale, wrapping up the events that absorbed his life "at least until September 1908, when I married and lived happily ever afterwards." Characteristically, he preferred the bold and romantic version of history to the more complicated truth. Winston and Clementine had a difficult marriage, in large part because Winston was such a demanding husband.

They had very different natures: Winston was free-spending, luxury-loving, inexhaustible; Clementine was austere, high-strung, a perfectionist who often became depressed and agitated. They had different tastes in people, in hobbies, in the hours they kept, in the holidays they enjoyed. Soon after they married, they stopped sharing a bedroom ("Breakfast should be had in bed, alone," said

Winston), and Clementine often went to sleep hours before her husband.

Winston's commitment to the marriage never wavered. Their daughter Mary, however, reports that Clementine did briefly fall in love with another man in 1935. On a yacht cruise without her husband, she had a romance with a fellow passenger, but it ended when they returned. Clementine suggested another trip, but her husband wouldn't permit it.

As time passed, the two spent more and more time apart. Winston loved to spend time at their country house, Chartwell, but Clementine disliked it: Winston had bought

Winston and Clementine, a week before their marriage in September 1908. This photograph is the first known picture of them together.

it without consulting her, and she never forgave him for it. She visited mostly on weekends and took long trips apart from her family. The two generally took separate vacations. As Churchill biographer Roy Jenkins observed, "it was almost incredible how Clementine managed to be absent at nearly all the most important moments of Churchill's life." Winston apparently didn't much object.

Clementine kisses Winston on his return to London from a week's visit to the United States in May 1959.

25

CHURCHILL'S ISLAND STORY

His Myth

"There is some one Myth for every man," wrote William Butler Yeats, "which, if we but knew it, would make us understand all that he did and thought." Churchill's myth was England. He described it in A History of the English-Speaking Peoples: *the longbow, bastard sons, trial by battle, soldiers on horseback. Only by considering Churchill's vision of the Island story can we understand the moral and historical framework through which he viewed events in his own time.*

All his life, Churchill was dazzled by the splendor of England. He loved its traditions and landscapes, its ordered hierarchies, its sailing ships and cottage homes. He had an emotional, even mystical, faith in its power.

Churchill offered his version of his country's past in *A History of the English-Speaking Peoples,* in which he explained how English institutions arose from time, battle, and tradition. His account neglected religion, literature, art, philosophy, economics, and science to dwell on politics and war, the aspects of history that preoccupied him.

Churchill praised England as the foundation of all that was best in society and government, and yet some of his most decided views contradicted its professed political ideals. For one thing, despite his respect for Parliament and representative government, Churchill was an ardent royalist. For his loyal soul, England and all its glory were embodied in the Crown. With a veneration that seems archaic, after meeting a two-year-old Princess Elizabeth in September 1928, he wrote, "She has an air of authority and reflectiveness astonishing in an infant." Clementine confided "that she thought [Winston] to be the last believer in the Divine Right of Kings: she felt reasonably sure the King was not." Churchill, however, didn't allow his showy reverence for his sovereign to interfere with his championship of other political principles.

More difficult to reconcile are Churchill's paeans to liberty and his bitter fight to maintain Britain's grip on its colonies, especially India. He glorified British political traditions—how, then, did he justify keeping India a subject nation? With Roosevelt, Churchill signed the Atlantic Charter—endorsing the "right of all peoples to choose the form of government under which they will live"—but immediately denied that the document applied to India.

This contradiction—seeming to exalt freedom while promoting unfreedom—didn't exist in Churchill's mind, because he held to a single goal: the glory of England. *Naught shall make us rue, if England to itself do rest but true.* Churchill revered his sovereign as the personification of English history. Churchill held to the Empire because England, tiny in land and population, needed its possessions to secure its place among nations. Churchill was never one of those who pretended that the British were in India purely out of kindness, that they endured voluntary exile for the welfare of the natives. For Churchill, India was Britain's indispensable prop, and this reality dictated the proper policies. Without India, without its vast Empire, England wasn't much more than an outcropping off the northern coast of Europe (after all, Britain and Ireland together amount to less than 125,000 square miles). Therefore, Churchill maintained that India was not the proper inheritor of English freedoms—at least, not yet.

But within his lifetime, Churchill's version of the Island story came to an end. He didn't realize it immediately. Consider his stubborn insistence on giving English pronunciation to foreign names, as he argued to the Foreign Office in 1945. He adopted a joking tone but in fact was dead serious when he declared that the names of foreign cities should not be pronounced to suit "the whims of foreigners living in those parts." This memo reveals just how out of touch Churchill was by the end of the war. He didn't understand that political reality, and the popular mood, required him to be more accommodating of the non-British point of view.

As Churchill watched, the world he knew disappeared. When he was born, the bearer of the title Duke of Marlborough held immense authority and prestige; by the

end of Churchill's life, the current Duke had opened
Blenheim Palace to the public and was complaining about
the consequent wear on his carpets. Churchill had been alive
when Queen Victoria was declared Empress of India in 1877
and when the Viceroy's House employed six thousand servants, and he was still alive when King George VI relin-
quished his Indian title and dropped the "I" for Emperor of
India from his royal signature. He watched as power—and
with the power, much pageantry—were swept away. What
alarmed Churchill was that few seemed to see clearly, or
mind much, what was being lost—*he* was not, he declared,
one of those who "on waking up in the morning wonder
what part of the British Empire could be given away during
the day."

In one of his most important speeches, Churchill vowed,
"We shall defend our Island, whatever the cost may be."
Churchill's Island—whose advancement was at the heart of
all he did—was not the actual Britain, smaller than Oregon,
with its General Strike, abdicating king, rioting Indians,
Labour Party, or slackening grasp on the Empire. It was
Shakespeare's island:

This royal throne of kings, this scepter'd isle,
This earth of majesty, this seat of Mars,
This other Eden, demi-paradise,
This fortress built by Nature for herself
Against infection and the hand of war,
This happy breed of men, this little world,

This precious stone set in the silver sea,
Which serves it in the office of a wall,
Or as a moat defensive to a house,
Against the envy of less happier lands,
This blessed plot, this earth, this realm, this England.

Churchill had his medals, his plumed hats, his ancestral portraits, horses stamping at the touch of his reins. This wasn't the diminished England, confined to an island, but an England imperial, expansive, and traditional. Of course it must end. But he refused to believe it.

26

CHURCHILL IN PHOTOGRAPHS

How He Changed Through Time

No matter how vivid a biography, we also demand to see pictures; words can't substitute for an actual look at a subject. It's not clear what we think we learn from seeing a person's face and watching it change over time, but it's clear we crave to do so. For this desire, photographs, with their detail and apparent scientific accuracy, are more satisfying than painted portraits.

A two-year-old Churchill leans against his mother, Jennie. Later, he would recall that she shone for him as a child like the "Evening Star."

With his sailor suit, Churchill, aged seven, wears a surprisingly supercilious expression for such a young child.

1895. Churchill, a subaltern, in the ornate full-dress uniform of the Fourth Hussars.

Churchill, a flying enthusiast, stands beside an early aircraft with Clementine in 1914. As First Lord of the Admiralty, Churchill introduced an Air Arm into the Navy.

In July 1925, Churchill is dressed for a polo match between the House of Commons and the House of Lords (Churchill's team won). Churchill continued to play polo until he was more than fifty years old.

1939. Churchill confers with the main proponent of the appeasement policy, Prime Minister Neville Chamberlain.

September 1940. Winston and Clementine inspect bomb damage to London docks. This famous picture was one of their family's favorites.

November 1964. On the eve of his ninetieth birthday, dressed in a green velvet siren suit, Churchill greets well-wishers from his window.

September 1940. Churchill—an instantly recognizable silhouette—reviews wartime defenses of England.

August 1941. Roosevelt and Churchill lead hymn singing during divine service aboard HMS Prince of Wales, *when the two world leaders met secretly at Placentia Bay.*

August 1941. Back in England, Churchill acknowledges the farewell cheers of the crew of HMS Prince of Wales.

Soon after returning from his meeting with President Roosevelt, Churchill for the first time brandishes the "V for victory."

February 1945. The "Big Three" at Yalta share a moment of jovial informality. Their casual air hides the dissension, which worsens as peace nears.

On the evening of victory, May 8, 1945, upon his return from Buckingham Palace, Churchill addresses a huge crowd: "In all our long history we have never seen a greater day than this." *Two months later, Churchill would be voted out of office.*

In Berlin, July 1945, amid the wreck of Hitler's chancellery,
Churchill's Russian guides show him Hitler's smashed chair.

January 1950. A seventy-five-year-old Churchill paints a scene in
Funchal, Madeira.

*April 1955. Churchill holds the door for the Queen as she leaves
10 Downing Street after attending a small dinner. This was Churchill's
last night as Prime Minister.*

*1965. After a service commemorating the twenty-fifth anniversary of the Battle of
Britain victory, Queen Elizabeth unveils a memorial stone to Churchill in
Westminster Abbey. Clementine and family stand beside pilots who fought in that
battle. The marble tablet reads, "Remember Winston Churchill."*

27

CHURCHILL AS THE HERO OF A NOVEL

The Imagined and the Real

A life doesn't make a good story: it's messy, themeless, with a predictable beginning and end. Nevertheless, readers of biography expect not only the discipline and reality of truth but also the artistry of novels.

Many of the most successful biographers make their subjects into almost fictional characters, with motives, symbols, motifs. ("A human life is always made up of a number of such motifs," ventured André Maurois, who found a flower motif in Disraeli's life; "when you study one of them, it will soon begin to impress itself upon you with a remarkable force." Ordered this way, the subject's life becomes consistent and meaningful.

This kind of biography is very satisfying—but is it more like fiction, with particular facts weighted to supply plot, unity, and moral? Like fiction, in which someone's imagination has imposed a pleasing shapeliness on the messy stuff of life?—a shapeliness that may or may not be true. And yet generally this is the kind of biography that seems most true.

The impulse to turn Churchill into a literary character is almost irresistible. The facts of his life adapt so easily to the devices of fiction: irony, suspense, paradox, foreshadowing, reversal, allusion, heightened diction, desperate causes, even witty banter. His story has a remarkable artfulness, so beautiful in design with its portents, symbols, and themes: it is these qualities that have etched Churchill the hero so deeply in memory. (Of course, Churchill himself encouraged his transformation. His cigars, his phrases, all simplified himself for public sight.)

In fact, Winston Churchill, the fictional character, would be unconvincing; the rich episodes of his history aren't lifelike. When a young Churchill asks for a dog, what novelist would be so unsubtle as to write that Winston demanded a bulldog—as he did? Or who, after Freud, could invent a hero, neglected by his mother and disdained by his father, who called his beloved nanny "Woom"? This extraordinarily literary—that is, constructed—quality to Churchill's life helps explain its deep resonance in the public mind. Literary flourishes are not historical facts, and yet the mind seizes on them; and somehow that Churchill loved whiskey or that he wept in public seems to convey as much as a chapter from his official biography. Real life is often less real than fiction, but the facts of Churchill's life penetrate with all the intensity of an allegory.

There is something melodramatic—legendary—fantastic about Churchill, a figure galloping out of the past. Even his name has a Dickensian aptness: sacred and lofty, with decisive, alliterative elements. Can the facts be true? Could he really have been a man who was not only a prominent world statesman but also rode to hounds, fenced, flew airplanes, played polo, owned racehorses, painted, farmed, and collected tropical fish? Who, without a university education, was a celebrated war correspondent, novelist, historian, and biographer—whose books were not only best-sellers but also won their author the Nobel Prize in literature, in the same year, it might be added, he accepted the Order of the Garter? He was the only person to serve in the War Cabinet in both World War I and World War II; he served in the Army, Navy, and Air Force. At Sandhurst, he'd learned how to ride bareback and to mount and dismount a trotting horse. At age seventy, in a shooting contest with General Eisenhower and guards officers, Churchill hit nine shots in the center of a bull's-eye and one on the fringe.

The story of Churchill's life is weighted with heavy-handed dramatic ironies: Churchill's father raging about his son's "total worthlessness"; Churchill writing in despair in the 1930s, "My career is a failure; it is finished. There is nothing more to offer"; and on May 21, 1940, just days after Churchill had become Prime Minister, an MP predicting, "Winston won't last five months! Opposition from Tories is already beginning." These pronouncements gratify the reader with the thrill of an impending reversal. Other prophecies came true: Harold Nicolson wrote, "He is a man who leads forlorn hopes, and when the hopes of England become forlorn, he will once again be summoned to leadership"; when asked in the late 1930s whether she thought Churchill would ever be Prime Minister, Clementine answered, "No, unless some great disaster were to sweep the country, and no one could wish for that"; on October 24, 1940, Churchill said as people cheered him, "I represent to them something which they whole-heartedly support: the determination to win. For a year or two they will cheer me," and as it happened, a few years later, those admiring crowds voted him out of office. The pleasure given by Churchill's story is all the greater, without the distraction of real suspense.

At the dramatic moments of Churchill's life, supporting characters also obligingly deliver their lines with cinematic flourish or arrange themselves in symbolical tableaux. After Churchill's humiliating ejection from office after the Dardanelles debacle, his longtime critic Field Marshal Lord Kitchener pronounced, "There is one thing at any rate they cannot take from you. The Fleet was ready." Decades later, on August 16, 1939, Churchill visited France's Maginot line and, in typical Churchill fashion, drove within shouting distance of Nazi troops on the Rhine's far side. Near them was a sign: EIN VOLK, EIN REICH, EIN FÜHRER. On the French bank: LIBERTÉ, ÉGALITÉ, FRATERNITÉ. On May 10, 1940, the day that Churchill would become the wartime Prime Minister, he received the simple note, "His Majesty the King wishes to see you at six P.M." Ordinary life rarely supplies these climactic moments, but in Churchill's life, they were commonplace.

Churchill even spoke like the leading character from a Noël Coward play, as he tossed out witty lines that sound too good to be true. When Lady Astor snapped, "Winston, if I were your wife, I'd put poison in your coffee," he retorted, "Nancy, if I were your husband, I'd drink it." In 1939, after reading a memo from Admiral Pound, Churchill expressed his disagreement with a single word—"Pennywise." He remarked that Ramsey MacDonald possessed "the gift of compressing the largest number of words into the smallest amount of thought."

Churchill biographers—like all biographers—decide their stories and include facts to support them. Someone portraying Churchill as the savior of his country chooses certain facts; someone debunking the Churchill myth chooses others. In deciding what facts to relate—where each detail must stand in for hundreds of omitted details—biographers act like novelists, using theme, irony, motif, metonymy, description, symbolism, morals, and the like to shape a particular image of their subject.

This shaping is easy, because merely mentioning a fact freights it with meaning: a gesture becomes suggestive, an incident turns symbolic. The telling detail has awesome power. That Churchill wore pale pink silk underwear suggests one view of the man; that he shot several men in the face at close range, another; that he loved butterflies, another. By using these devices, biographers give their subjects the reassuring coherence associated with fiction. Biographers must be accurate, of course, but the very facts that restrict them allow them to invent.

A biographer with a flair for symbols could exploit the fact that Churchill loved champagne and Hitler hated champagne; or that near the end of World War II, Churchill peed on the Siegfried line; or that he owned an American Indian chief's feathered warbonnet, bloodstained and hung with scalps. Despite his reverence for Empire, he never visited Australia or New Zealand and never set foot in India after 1898. He opposed allowing television cameras inside Westminster Abbey for Queen Elizabeth's coronation ceremony. He enjoyed playing pinball and cheated when he could. He loved gambling, picnics, card games, swimming and turning somersaults in his pool at Chartwell, and driving at high speeds. He bred racehorses and registered under his father's racing colors, chocolate and pink, and was elected to the Jockey Club. He disliked freshly squeezed orange juice; the smell of wax; the sounds of whistling, cowbells clanging, loud voices, ticking clocks, or telephones ringing. He was so bored by the movie *Citizen Kane* that he walked out. Churchill rarely went to church, but he did enjoy christenings; he traced his American roots back to two forebears who fought against the British in the Revolutionary War and to an Iroquois woman; the "most overworked word" in his vocabulary, according to his secretary, was "prod."

Imagined with the help of fiction's devices, Churchill sometimes seems less a personality than a personification of a theme: the ancient fighting soul of the British. (It's true that Churchill is romanticized in memory; he *strove* to be ro-

manticized.) But he can't be allowed to dissolve into archetype; it's more extraordinary that he actually lived.
Churchill's story, remembered in the trappings of art,
achieves mythic scale. How could his story be true? Yet it
was.

28

CHURCHILL'S DESTINY

How He Saw Himself

*To understand Churchill, we must understand how he viewed him-
self: a man chosen by Fate to achieve a noble destiny. And while we
might scoff at his superstitious egoism, there's the inescapable fact
that, looking at his life, he does appear to have been a man chosen
by Fate to achieve a noble destiny. His American mother, his injured
shoulder, the rider on the pale horse, the telegram sent by the general, the years in the wilderness, the reckless vow to fight to the
end—all played their part.*

For many great figures, the path to success rises gradually upward, as they overcome temporary obstacles to arrive at their
peak. Not for Churchill. His jagged career mixed great successes with seemingly insurmountable reverses. Falling from
office after the Dardanelles, during the isolation of the wilderness years, after the shocking defeat in 1945—Churchill some-

how fought his way back into a public role each time. It was his absolute faith in his great destiny that allowed him to persevere against setbacks that would have defeated most people.

At the same time that Churchill believed destiny was preserving him to fulfill some historic role, however, he was also haunted by a premonition that he'd die before he could fulfill his ambitions. Asked why he expected to die young, he explained that his father had died at age forty-six. This was a powerful combination for a leader: a sense of invulnerability, of election, and also of burning urgency.

Trust in his destiny made Churchill fearless. He wrote to his mother in 1897, while he was still in uniform, "I am so conceited I do not believe the Gods would create so potent a being as myself for so prosaic an ending." Decades later, he wrote to his wife from the trenches, "Above all don't be worried about me. If my destiny has not been already accomplished I shall be guarded surely."

Churchill can perhaps be excused for his credulity. Even putting aside his survival of the normal risks of the battlefield and of prosaic geriatric health problems, Churchill withstood mortal danger a surprising number of times.

Twice, in March 1886 and again in 1943, he fought dangerous bouts of pneumonia.

At age eighteen, playing tag, Churchill jumped from a bridge thirty feet from the ground; he tried to grab a treetop but fell. He ruptured his kidney, was unconscious for three days, and received a spine injury that gave him a slight stoop for the rest of his life.

Only a few months later, he nearly drowned during a holiday in Switzerland.

In 1899, aged twenty-five, he helped to rescue an armored train under attack by enemy fire and was captured by the Boers. He soon escaped from the war camp and, with a price on his head, managed to make his way to safety.

While still in South Africa, he was thrown by his bolting horse as Boer riflemen drew near. A mounted British scout on a pale horse appeared just in time—"Death in Revelation, but life to me!"—and Churchill mounted up beside him and rode to safety.

Not long after, as a commissioned officer disguised in civilian clothes, he carried an urgent military report through Johannesburg. If he'd been stopped and searched, he'd have been shot where he stood.

Just a week after arriving at the front in 1915, Churchill received a telegram from a general requesting a meeting. When Churchill returned after walking for miles in the mud, angry because the meeting hadn't actually taken place, he learned that his shelter had been destroyed by a shell five minutes after he'd left it.

Characteristically eager to tackle any challenge, Churchill took up flying and survived several near misses in early airplanes. One plane caught fire; another flipped after takeoff; another crashed after the guiding stick failed. He finally ended his lessons after a crash landing seriously injured his flight instructor.

At age fifty-seven, in 1931, he suffered serious injuries after being hit by a car on Fifth Avenue, in New York City.

Brushes with death never cowed Churchill. When a sniper shot at him during a 1944 visit to Greece, Churchill's reaction was to exclaim, "Cheek!"

Churchill believed himself chosen by destiny. When he became Prime Minister in 1940, he reflected on how the circumstances of his birth, his abilities, and the quirks of his political fortunes had uniquely fitted him to fill his great station: "I was conscious of a profound sense of relief. At last I had the authority to give directions over the whole scene. I felt as if I were walking with Destiny, and that all my past life had been but a preparation for this hour and for this trial." Churchill felt that his American mother—a descendant of a lieutenant in George Washington's army—gave him a special understanding of the "great Republic," and he wrote of the Anglo-American alliance, "It certainly was odd that it should all work out this way; and once again I had the feeling . . . of being used, however unworthy, in some appointed plan."

As Churchill himself noticed, even seemingly chance events played their role. He reflected on the 1896 accident that dislocated his shoulder and prevented him from using a sword; the injury bothered him until he died but perhaps also saved his life.

You never can tell whether bad luck may not after all turn out to be good luck. Perhaps if in the charge of Omdurman I had been able to use a sword, instead of having to adopt a modern weapon like a Mauser pistol, my story might not have got so far as the telling. One must never forget when misfortunes come that it is quite possible they are saving one from something much worse; or that when you make some great mistake, it may very easily serve you better than the best-advised decision.

In the same disguise, Churchill's banishment to the political wilderness during the 1930s was lucky. He'd warned of the dangers; he'd been ignored and scorned; in 1940, he bore no responsibility. As Churchill explained later, "I could not be reproached either for making the war or with want of preparation for it"—or, as he put it more poetically, "Over me beat the invisible wings."

These invisible wings did more than preserve him from death or political extinction. They covered him with unexpected favors: the rare chance in South Africa to make himself a hero, where by pure luck during his prison escape, he knocked at the one British door for twenty miles; the perfectly timed inheritance from a distant relative that provided the money to buy Chartwell; the 1938 bailout from the rich admirer that allowed him to be a candidate for Prime Minister in 1940.

It was under the invisible wings that Churchill was chosen to be wartime Prime Minister. It happened in the afternoon of May 9, 1940, at a meeting at 10 Downing Street to choose Chamberlain's successor, if he couldn't continue as Prime Minister. Chamberlain faced the two contenders: Halifax and Churchill. They didn't know it, of course, but within hours Hitler would unleash a brutal attack in western Europe.

By the end of the meeting, the choice was made. This decision—Churchill as Prime Minister—blazes from the mass

of facts, and yet most accounts of May 1940 accept, with surprising docility, the certainty of this outcome. But it was
hardly inevitable.

If Foreign Secretary Lord Halifax had pushed for the job,
there is little doubt he would have got it. In Churchill's favor
was the fact that his support was growing in the House. But
resigning Prime Minister Chamberlain, and the bulk of the
Conservative Party he led, wanted Halifax. The King wanted
Halifax. The Labour leadership would have accepted Halifax.
True, the fact that Halifax was a peer presented a hurdle, but
that could have been solved. Nevertheless, Halifax bowed
out.

Why did Halifax defer to Churchill? Those in high office
seek higher office, and Halifax—a haughty man of terrific
ambition—was no exception. It wasn't that he wanted to
leave government: he remained in the Cabinet as an out-
spoken Foreign Secretary. It wasn't that he didn't have an
opinion about the proper course for Britain: he persistently
argued that Britain must consider a negotiated peace. Did he
shrink from bearing so much responsibility? Unlikely, given
a career that included several high posts; in the one he'd most
enjoyed, Viceroy of India, he'd decided the fates of more
than 300 million. Did he lack the stomach to be Prime
Minister with a restive Churchill under him, speechifying
and criticizing at every turn? Perhaps. Perhaps he believed
he'd be better able to restrain Churchill's wilder ideas if he
remained Foreign Secretary, or perhaps he predicted, as
many did, that Churchill's government would soon fail and
that he could then replace Churchill with that powerful

adversary removed. Or perhaps he truly believed that Churchill, not he, had the qualities needed to lead the country. Whatever his reason, Halifax did refuse the highest political prize when it was within his grasp.

It was Halifax's habit, when offered high office, to demur until his superiors pleaded that his service was indispensable. If Chamberlain had insisted that it was Halifax's patriotic duty to assume the Premiership at this critical hour, Halifax perhaps would have done so, whatever his hesitations. (Halifax certainly performed his greatest service by declining the office. This was a man who on May 10, 1940—having learned upon waking that, at dawn, Hitler had attacked Belgium and Holland on a path to France, at a time when the British leadership was in crisis—nevertheless left the Foreign Office to keep his *dentist's* appointment.)

If Halifax might have accepted the position had Chamberlain insisted, the question becomes, why didn't Chamberlain press Halifax harder? He said he preferred Halifax, and it would have been only natural for him to feel that way. Halifax had loyally supported him while Churchill had opposed him. And yet instead of continuing to push Halifax, Chamberlain turned to Churchill. *Why*?

Chamberlain prided himself that he was realistic, businesslike, with a passionate dedication to peace. He had all these qualities—and these identical defects. With his narrow, prosaic mind, and in his vanity, Chamberlain simply couldn't comprehend Hitler. Even as of September 30, 1940, he complained in a letter to the King that his failed attempts to avoid war "might well have succeeded if they had not come up against the insatiate and inhuman ambitions of a fanatic." Wasn't that the *point* of all who criticized Chamberlain's policy? That he'd persisted in his appeasement with utter disregard for Hitler's obvious nature? Perhaps, at long last, Chamberlain grasped that his virtues (which were also Halifax's) were out of season and that it was Churchill who possessed the necessary qualities of imagination and stomach for war. And of course, it was Churchill who embodied—for the British people and for the Germans as well—a policy of absolute resistance to Hitler.

Churchill trusted that destiny would guide and protect him. "Chance, Fortune, Luck, Destiny, Fate, Providence seem to me only different ways of expressing the same thing, to wit, that a man's own contribution to his life story is continually dominated by an external superior power." And yet . . . Churchill's good fortune was also bad fortune. He would win a great victory, and fulfill his destiny, but not as he expected—and not as he wanted.

29

CHURCHILL THE IMPERIALIST

His Cause

Most people live personal, domestic lives; few devote themselves to a great cause. Early in his life, Churchill settled on his purpose, and he never wavered from it: "I want to see the British Empire preserved . . . in its strength and splendor." Most of what he did—both good and bad—sprang from his desire to maintain the Empire. Sometimes, he was praised for what he did in the Empire's name, and at other times, abused.

For the first several decades of his life, just as Churchill's position in the world expanded, so did the British Empire's. In 1900, Churchill was a newly elected MP, and the Empire was the largest the world had ever seen; after World War I, Churchill was one of the Empire's leaders as it stretched to its widest palmy reach. Churchill's purpose—what he fought for his whole life—was its advancement.

Born into the ruling elite, Churchill never doubted his fitness to command, and he expected every class and race to accept its lot cheerfully. "I was brought up in that state of civilization," he explained, "when it was everywhere accepted that men are born unequal."

At home in England, Churchill wanted to improve the lives of the poor and unfortunate—but from a lordly instinct of benevolence, not from a belief that his fellow Britons were entitled to certain rights and protections. He wanted to improve the old order, not create a new one. He reacted harshly to demands, to threats, to strikes (whether by suffragettes, miners, nationalists, or unions); he gave out of condescending generosity, not out of obligation, to his good, loyal people.

These same beliefs, on a larger scale, shaped Churchill's attitudes toward colonial subjects. He never doubted that the British, with their genius for government, should shoulder the burden of governing their inferiors in foreign parts. He was untroubled by the Empire's double nature: for whites, democratic and free; for nonwhites, authoritarian and military. He took an unabashedly racial view of the matter: the superior white had a *duty* and a *right* to rule. In 1922, he wrote the Governor of Bengal's wife:

I am sure . . . you will do your best to keep the Flag flying and the prestige and authority of the white man undiminished. Our true duty in India lies to those 300 millions whose lives and means of existence would be squandered if entrusted to the chatterboxes who are supposed to speak for India today.

Even during the Second World War, while Indian soldiers fought to defend Britain, Churchill carefully distinguished between races. He wrote the Secretary of State for War to protest the fact that two British brigades went by the name of the "36th Indian Division"—a circumstance which he considered to go "below the level of grovelling to which we have been subject." In 1943, he asked, "Why be apologetic about Anglo-Saxon superiority? We are superior." Later, he explained, "When you learn to think of a race as inferior beings it is difficult to get rid of that way of thinking; when I was a subaltern the Indian did not seem to me equal to the white man."

Churchill believed that the purpose of the overseas Empire was to support England's world stature, and in his imperial vision, India shone brightest. For generations, a tiny number of Britons (at peak, about 150,000) had controlled more than 300 million inhabitants of India, on a subcontinent larger than Europe. Churchill didn't want to see this arrangement changed, and he isolated himself in the 1930s by opposing even modest steps toward Indian self-government. Churchill argued that Britain had brought India a civilization "far above anything they could possibly have achieved themselves or could maintain" and prophesied that the "false benevolence" of granting independence to India would result in chaos, blood, and famine as well as the undermining of Britain's world-power status. He condemned those who supported self-rule. "It is alarming and also nauseating to see Mr. Gandhi," scoffed Churchill in a 1931 speech, "now posing as a fakir of a type well-known in the East, striding half-naked up the steps of the Vice-Regal Palace. . . . Such a spectacle can only increase the unrest in India and the danger to which white people there are exposed." (Who was the Viceroy who was willing to meet with Gandhi? Lord Halifax, in an earlier incarnation.)

Another major effort by Churchill on the Empire's behalf was his wartime cultivation of Roosevelt, whose aid was crucial to British victory. Churchill—who never stopped talking, who never listened to anyone else, who excelled at biting criticism—managed to hold his tongue, except to praise and wheedle. "No lover," Churchill said, "ever studied every whim of his mistress as I did those of President Roosevelt." By careful correspondence, several face-to-face meetings (Churchill did most of the traveling), characteristic eloquence, and uncharacteristic tact, Churchill worked to build American support for Britain. He didn't enjoy playing the role of supplicant, but he did what he had to do. In July 1940, as Nazis stormed across Europe, opposed only by Britain, Churchill begged Roosevelt to send destroyers— with dignity, of course, but still he begged: "Mr. President, with great respect I must tell you that in the long history of the world this is a thing to do *now*." He left many harsh things unsaid—letters rewritten, speeches softened. He did it for the Empire.

Given Churchill's intense pride in the British Empire, it's surprising to learn his hopes for the postwar relationship of Britain and the United States: he repeatedly, and approvingly, predicted that they'd unite—he anticipated common citizenship and the "dollar sterling." His well-publicized friendship with Roosevelt was meant to symbolize the deep affinity of their two countries. In his famous "Iron Curtain" speech of March 5, 1946, Churchill joined the two countries together in rhetoric:

> The United States stands at this time at the pinnacle of world power. . . . Opportunity is here now, clear and shining for both our countries. . . . It is necessary that constancy of mind, persistency of purpose and the grand simplicity of decision shall guide and rule the conduct of the English-speaking peoples in peace as they did in war.

But why would Churchill, who fought so fiercely to preserve the British Empire, welcome the prospect of melding with the United States?

The answer might also explain why, when the time came, contrary to expectations, he made no real effort as Opposition party leader after 1945 to defeat the Attlee government's policy in favor of Indian independence.

He hoped to build *another* Empire, a stronger one. He foresaw that the existing Empire, based on India, was doomed. Once India left, the rest of the Empire would collapse as well. But just as the Indian Empire had once replaced the American Empire, now the United States could replace India. And what a partner! The United States was at the pinnacle of world power. In his August 16, 1945, address to the House of Commons, in a discussion of the use of the atomic bomb, Churchill addressed this preeminence:

The United States stand at this moment at the summit of the world. I rejoice that this should be so. Let them act up to the level of their power and their responsibility, not for themselves but for others, for all men in all lands, and then a brighter day may dawn upon human history.

And for all his deference to the United States, in Churchill's view, Britain remained the senior partner of the two. After all, Churchill emphasized, America owed its best traditions to Britain—their shared language and the values of democracy, personal liberty, and the rule of law. He pointedly wrote, "The [United States's] Constitution was a reaffirmation of faith in the principles painfully evolved over the centuries by the English-speaking peoples. It enshrined longstanding English ideas of justice and liberty, henceforth to be regarded on the other side of the Atlantic as basically American."

The problem with this plan was that the United States didn't want to play that role and didn't see the future as Churchill saw it. As the years wore on, Churchill realized that, try as he might, he wouldn't live to see a great reunion.

India was lost and, after India, the rest of the Empire, and the United States wasn't to be gained. Churchill had dreaded this dwindling of British stature. He'd thundered in 1942, "I have not become the King's First Minister in order to preside over the liquidation of the British Empire." It was one of his life's ironies that, in fact, this was precisely his fate. *"We shall defend our Island,"* he'd pledged in 1940, *"whatever the cost may be."* The defense of the Island cost the Empire. Churchill's reverence for the Empire blinded him to its weak and overtaxed structure, and he didn't appreciate that the added strains of war would cripple it. And not only did Britain lack the resources to rule its Empire after the war— it had lost the desire to paint the map red. When peace came, the British wanted to come home, settle down, rebuild. The principle of self-rule had taken root in the world, and Britain accepted it, too. "It is with deep grief that I watch the clattering down of the British Empire," Churchill said in 1947. "Many have defended Britain against her foes. None can defend her against herself."

By the end of his life, Churchill had seen both the Empire's greatest expansion and its contraction into a damp island of some 45 million people. Churchill's cousin Clare Sheridan observed of him in a 1950 letter, "Of course he was depressed—says everything he has worked for all his life (the Brit. Emp.) has been thrown away by the socialists in power—he accused the U.S. of having been instrumental in breaking up our Colonial Empire." Years later, he told her, "In the end it has all been for nothing. . . . The Empire *I* believed in has gone."

But it wasn't until Churchill died in 1965 that the sun finally set on the Empire. His mere presence in the world, with his massive prestige and position, upheld the banner of Britain's former glory. His funeral marked its descent. The next most memorable occasion of British pageantry was the marriage of Charles, Prince of Wales, to Churchill's distant cousin, Lady Diana Spencer, in 1981. The world thrilled at the royal splendor: the glass coach bearing the bride to Saint Paul's Cathedral, the throngs of people cheering in the streets, Diana murmuring, "I, Diana Frances, take thee, Philip Charles Arthur George" (in the wrong order—his first name is Charles). But how different everything was. The Empire had been swept away. The royal pomp had become a tourist attraction, and though splendid, the ceremony seemed overdone, performed by such a diminished nation.

30

CHURCHILL'S EMPIRE
How He Saw the World

Understanding where *the biography's subject lived is as important as understanding* when. *Churchill considered himself to live in England, but more important, in the capital of the British Empire. It's easy, given the Britain of today, to forget the immensity of the Empire at its height, when London directed the government of more than one-quarter of the world's land and population. Churchill was alive when the Empire's reach was greatest, and its supreme position matched the enormity of his own ambitions. He never resigned himself to its diminishment.*

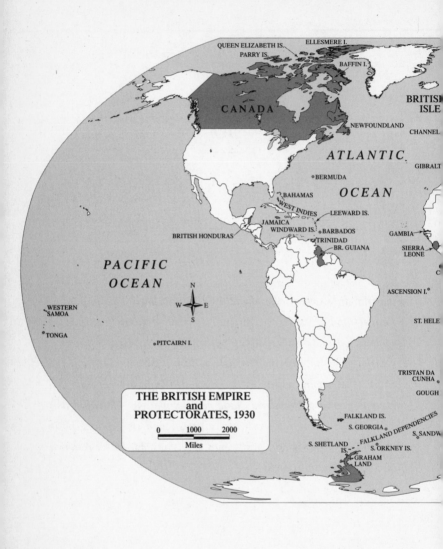

THE BRITISH EMPIRE
and
PROTECTORATES, 1930

0   1000   2000

Miles

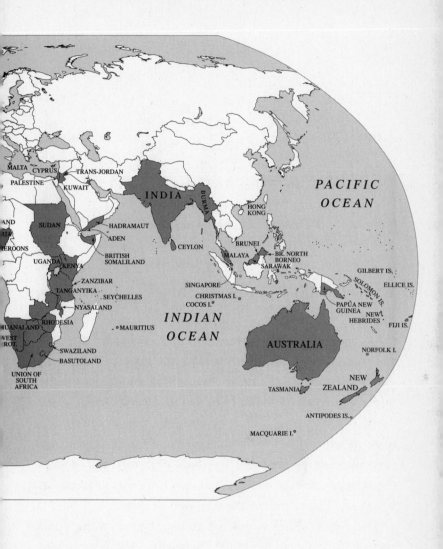

MALTA
CYPRUS
TRANS-JORDAN
PALESTINE
KUWAIT
INDIA
BURMA
HONG KONG
PACIFIC OCEAN
...AND
...RIA
SUDAN
HADRAMAUT
ADEN
...EROONS
UGANDA
KENYA
BRITISH SOMALILAND
CEYLON
BRUNEI
MALAYA
BR. NORTH BORNEO
SARAWAK
GILBERT IS.
SOLOMON IS.
ELLICE IS.
ZANZIBAR
TANGANYIKA
SEYCHELLES
SINGAPORE
CHRISTMAS I.
COCOS I.
PAPUA NEW GUINEA
NEW HEBRIDES
FIJI IS.
NYASALAND
INDIAN OCEAN
...HUANALAND
...WEST ...ROT.
RHODESIA
MAURITIUS
SWAZILAND
BASUTOLAND
AUSTRALIA
NORFOLK I.
UNION OF SOUTH AFRICA
NEW ZEALAND
TASMANIA
ANTIPODES IS.
MACQUARIE I.

31

CHURCHILL AND ROOSEVELT

Friends as Well as Allies?

Winston Churchill and Franklin Roosevelt Had a Warm Friendship

Churchill and Roosevelt were bound together by affection and respect. Each delighted to share the stage of world history with another of similar outsize abilities. As Roosevelt wrote Churchill, "It is fun to be in the same decade as you." They shared many common interests: the war, of course; the navy, in which they had both served and which remained a particular interest for both; the study of history and biography; the pleasures of country and city. Each was an aristocrat who sought to represent the common people.

Their relationship embodied and strengthened the bond between Britain and the United States. In 1939, even before Churchill became Prime Minister, Roosevelt initiated a remarkable correspondence that continued until Roosevelt's death. They exchanged more than seventeen hundred messages, carried on running jokes, and even exchanged poems.

Churchill gladly pursued the relationship with the American president; he recognized from the beginning that Britain's victory, and perhaps even survival, depended on the United States's support. Roosevelt, for his part, acknowledged that Britain was holding the line against Nazi Germany at a time when the American public opposed entering the war.

Churchill's cultivation of Roosevelt was particularly critical for Britain in the period before the United States entered the war in December 1941. In September 1940, Roosevelt consummated the destroyers-for-bases deal, in which U.S. destroyers were exchanged for use of British Atlantic bases, and in March 1941, the United States under Lend-Lease began to "lend" military equipment to cash-poor Britain—a Roosevelt policy hailed by Churchill as "the most unsordid act in the history of any nation." Churchill and Roosevelt's dramatic meeting at sea in August 1941 demonstrated to the world that the two English-speaking countries had a "special relationship." Churchill was so determined that this first critical wartime meeting go well that, to prepare for the divine service planned for combined American and British crews, he conducted a full rehearsal aboard HMS *Prince of Wales* while it was on its way to the Atlantic Meeting. There, the two leaders signed the historic Atlantic Charter, a joint declaration of principles and aims. After Japan bombed Pearl Harbor and Hitler declared war, the two leaders became official allies.

Naturally, Churchill and Roosevelt didn't always agree. Despite occasional differences, however, a warm friendship bolstered their shared objectives and common ideals.

Winston Churchill and Franklin Roosevelt Did Not Have a Warm Friendship

The emotional Churchill couldn't resist the vision of the two leaders of the great English-speaking nations united as war comrades. He did feel some real affection for Roosevelt. Roosevelt, however, was more aloof, more pragmatic. He'd instantly disliked Churchill when he'd met him at the end of the First World War and was further irritated when Churchill let slip, at the Atlantic Meeting in August 1941, that he didn't remember that first meeting.

The two men needed each other. Both worked hard to grease their official relationship with the lubricant of camaraderie, to the point that sometimes their heartiness became treacly, as when Prime Minister Churchill signed himself "Former Naval Person" (a coy reference to his former post as First Lord, used to avoid the cold formality of his proper title and to emphasize their common ground). In truth, however, conflict shadowed their association. The two leaders clashed on important issues like imperialism, the speed of American entry into the war, Mediterranean strategy, the opening of the second front, military aid to China, and policy toward the Soviets. Roosevelt returned Churchill's gestures of personal friendship, but at the same time, he worked unsentimentally to undermine the British Empire and to strengthen the position of the United States.

The myth of their great friendship is due in part to Churchill's effusive praise for Roosevelt. Desperate for American support at every stage of the war, he wooed the President with public applause—but he was harsher in private. Away from the microphones, Churchill protested of Lend-Lease, Roosevelt's plan to allow the United States to supply Britain with war materials on credit, that "we are not only to be skinned, but flayed to the bone." His prediction was correct; the United States used Lend-Lease ruthlessly to strip Britain of its assets.

And perhaps Churchill, for all his protestations of affection, wasn't as fond of Roosevelt as he said, at least by the end. Without a convincing excuse, he decided not to attend Roosevelt's funeral in the spring of 1945, nor did he broadcast to the nation on the occasion. By not attending the funeral, Churchill also lost the chance to meet the new president, Harry Truman. Roosevelt had always been the dominant partner in the special relationship, and Churchill had traveled to Washington; with Roosevelt dead, Churchill may have wanted Truman to come to him, to move the seat of the Anglo-American relations to London. At bottom, the special relationship was a means to promote national interests.

32

CHURCHILL'S IMAGINATION

How He Saw History

A biography attempts to convey a personality, with its peculiar atmosphere and impulses. Churchill's personality, it happens, was dominated by his sense of English history.

"The fortunate generations are the homogeneous ones," Lytton Strachey commented, "those which begin and end, comfortably, within the boundaries of a single Age. It is the straddlers who are unlucky." Churchill was a straddler. The past, as he imagined it, fueled his powers. He looked backward to a vanished world—the world into which he'd been born—not to the future.

Churchill's faith in Britain and its destiny gave him his courage, his optimism, and his ambition. However, the traditional vision of Britain that fitted Churchill for his splendid achievements also divided him from the spirit of the age, and by the end of his life, he'd outlived his own time and the version of the Island story he cherished.

Churchill's affinity for history sprang, in part, from the tremendous changes he witnessed in his own life. He was born in 1874, when the Civil War general Ulysses Grant was U.S. president, before the use of electricity, the phonograph, the cinema, the typewriter, the telephone, the radio, or the automobile. In 1898, at Omdurman, he fought in the last British cavalry charge to use lances as weapons. In 1900, during his American lecture tour, Churchill was introduced by Mark Twain—who introduced him then as "the hero of five wars, the author of six books, and the future Prime Minister of Great Britain." When Churchill entered the House of Commons that year, not even a third of Britons were entitled to vote; he was forty-four years old before any woman could vote. He saw the apex of the British Empire, made strong and rich by the industrial revolution; these advances initially fortified England in its best defense, the ocean, but Churchill would live to see newer technology— first air power, then atomic power—overcome that protective moat.

To Churchill, the past seemed as immediate as the present. The places of his childhood reverberated with English history: the Vice-Regal Lodge in Dublin, Blenheim Palace, Harrow, London. "I can see myself . . . sitting a little boy," he told Harrow students, "always feeling the glory of England and its history, surrounding me and about me." He believed every prospective officer should read Plutarch's *Lives*. To denounce the Munich Agreement, he pointed to lessons from King Ethelred the Unready's reign. One evening in August 1940, when the Nazis threatened across the sea, Churchill

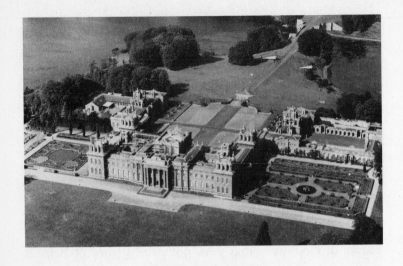

Blenheim Palace was the nation's gift to John Churchill, the first Duke of Marlborough, in thanks for his victories against the French in the early eighteenth century. Churchill was born at Blenheim and might have taken as his personal charge its Victory Column's inscription, describing the great Duke:

> The Hero not only of his Nation, but of his Age:
> Whose Glory was equal in the Council and in the Field;
> Who, by Wisdom, Justice, Candour, and Address,
> Reconcil'd various, and even opposite Interests;
> Acquired an Influence
> Which no Rank, no Authority can give,
> Nor any Force, but that of superior Virtue;
> Became the fixed important Center
> Which united, In one common Cause,
> The principal States of Europe. . . .
> When raised the highest, when exerted the most,
> Rescued the Empire from Desolation,
> Asserted and confirmed the Liberties of Europe.

told his colleagues, "I want to discuss the problems of invasion." They met that night expecting, reasonably enough, to discuss possible German attack; instead, they probed the challenges faced by William the Conqueror in 1066. In 1944, just before D-Day, Churchill asked for all the data on weather, time, and conditions when William had landed on English shores—again, he wanted to study this last successful invasion, even if it had taken place nearly nine hundred years before. This study of history allowed him to see what others missed. Few had shared his belief in Russia's ability to hold out against Germany in 1941; the Americans estimated that Russia would last only three months. Churchill argued he would bet that in two years' time, Russia would still be fighting. The generals should read about Napoleon and the 1812 retreat from Moscow.

Churchill's historical vision gave him a reverence for the traditional symbols of British power. Despite wartime distractions, he found time to admonish:

Prime Minister to First Lord   18.IX.40

   Surely you can run to a new Admiralty flag. It
grieves me to see the present dingy object every
morning.

When the Foreign Office proposed to plan the evacuation of the royal family, the Crown jewels, and the coronation chair, Churchill flatly refused. Legend foretold that if the apes on Gibraltar ever left, British rule there would end; in 1944, when Churchill learned that the apes' numbers were dropping, he ordered that every effort be made to keep at least twenty-four apes on Gibraltar. Apes' names and ages were recorded on the garrison muster, with births and deaths noted in the casualty lists.

Churchill's strong sense of history helped him in wartime, because he saw war's violent disruption as part of the normal progress of Britain. It also convinced him that, no matter how bleak the prospects, Britain would win in the end. So rather than mourn the loss of peace, Churchill rushed to play his part.

Churchill studied history, and he shaped it. As a consequence, he was preoccupied not only by the achievements of earlier generations but also by how later generations would judge his achievements. To establish his version of events, he wrote voluminous memoirs. "These are *my* story," he retorted to criticism of his World War II volumes. "If someone else likes to write *his* story, let him." All his books, in one way or another, told his own history. His reports from the field—books like *The River War, The Malakand Field Force, My Early Life*—were history as he'd seen it as a dashing young subaltern. His biographies, *Lord Randolph Churchill* and *Marlborough,* recast his forebears' records. Slightly more impersonally, in *A History of the English-Speaking Peoples,* Churchill filtered a vast history to teach his version of the Island story. He preferred the bold and simple; his sense of the past was too romantic, too vivid, to be strictly accurate. He strove to illuminate the development of the genius of the

English race, and in his mind, noble legends were as important as cold facts.

Churchill's most significant works, his memoirs of World Wars I and II, were history as seen by a world statesman. Churchill knew that the condition of enduring fame is harsh scrutiny, and he wrote these volumes to vindicate himself. "History will bear me out," he declared, "particularly as I shall write that history myself." He admitted that he exploited hindsight to "correct or bury" any mistakes, and he tweaked and even hid the truth when it suited him. Churchill ignored the contributions of those who had opposed or disappointed him—for example, he barely acknowledged the work of the Chief of the Imperial General Staff, Alan Brooke, with whom he battled constantly. Of the War Cabinet's critical decision to fight on alone during the early days of his Premiership, Churchill claimed:

> Future generations may deem it noteworthy that the supreme question of whether we should fight on alone never found a place upon the War Cabinet agenda. It was taken for granted and as a matter of course . . . and we were much too busy to waste time upon such academic, unreal issues.

This is simply untrue. Why would Churchill lie to hide the War Cabinet's debates on just that question? Out of generosity to Halifax; also, publishing this account in 1949, Churchill as Conservative leader had no reason to point out his party's defeatism in 1940; furthermore, Churchill wanted to emphasize the world's debt to Britain and so hid the fact that Britain had ever wavered in its high purpose. Churchill's war memoirs were not detached accounts but rather personal testimony.

To mold the impression of future generations, in his accounts Churchill depicted "Churchill" with the swashbuckling mannerisms and courtly language worthy of a hero. Of a 1942 visit to the desert front, he wrote, "We sallied forth early to see the prospective battlefield and the gallant troops who were to hold it." Few contemporaries would have described their movements as *sallying forth*. One of his much-studied wartime directives began, "Renown awaits the Commander who first . . ." and was known among his colleagues by the opening phrase, "Renown Awaits." His comrades-in-arms weren't always capable of the same gallant parlance. Consider this uneven exchange during the Battle of Alamein. Churchill wrote with elaborate courtesy to Air Chief Marshal Tedder to congratulate him on the "magnificent" fighting of his men, who were "playing a glorious part" in battle. In less heroic terms, Air Chief Marshal Tedder replied that they were indeed "determined to make a job of it." Always conscious of posterity's eye, and with a vision of himself as a hero in the enduring Island story, Churchill described himself as he wanted to be remembered.

Churchill worried about history's verdict, and he appealed to history's judgment. In July 1940, after France surrendered, and after the French naval commander at Oran refused to hand over or scuttle his warships, Churchill ordered that the

British navy sink the French ships so that they could not fall to the Nazis. More than a thousand French died. This violence against Britain's former ally shocked many, and Churchill himself wept when he announced the attack: "I leave the judgment of our action, with confidence, to Parliament. I leave it to the nation, and I leave it to the United States. I leave it to the world and history." Meeting with Stalin in October 1944, Churchill handed Stalin a sheet of paper, "the naughty document," which suggested percentages of British and Soviet predominance in Eastern Europe; Stalin ticked his approval. Mindful of future scrutiny, Churchill suggested, "Might it not be thought rather cynical if it seemed we had disposed of these issues, so fateful to millions of people, in such an offhand manner? Let us burn the paper." Stalin replied, "No, you keep it." (Far from burning it, obviously, Churchill published it.)

By supplying his own version of history, Churchill tried to define his time—and his place in it. But although he appears to be a supreme embodiment of his age, he was also outside it. His message to General Wavell about defending Singapore rings as an anachronism; he insisted that the battle must be fought to the last man to uphold the "honour of the British Empire" and the "reputation of our country and our race." Churchill tried to speak the timeless language of heroes and instead spoke out of the past; this heroic, histrionic language doesn't belong in 1942. His great speeches evoked the glories and traditions of bygone days—not the promises of the future.

Some personalities take their color from their age, while

others seem to belong properly to a different one. Perhaps, with his love for airplanes, radar, and automobiles, Churchill thought himself a man of the future. He wasn't. Churchill displayed the imperial spirit of the nineteenth century, with all its confidence, when Britain had been unrivaled.

Straddlers are unlucky. "Scarcely anything material or established which I was brought up to believe was permanent and vital, has lasted," reflected Churchill. "Everything I was sure or taught to be sure was impossible, has happened." He wrote that in 1930. The quality that the public revered in Churchill—his compelling vision of the heroic past—eventually led them to dismiss him as a historical relic. Churchill lived into an age in which the values he defended—of social tradition, soldierly glory, and British superiority—were undermined. His certainty didn't suit his age of change and doubt. At the moment of his country's forlorn hope, his traditional qualities, braced by his imagination, became once again necessary, and he led the country to victory. But he quickly went out of fashion again, afterward.

33

Churchill and Hitler

Nemesis

Most great figures are remembered singly—not Churchill. He's always framed with his great adversary, Hitler. Juxtaposition highlights certain facts and obscures others, though not always in predictable ways. Consider the two men: one was cheerful, witty, and magnanimous; the other was humorless, cruel, a hypochondriac; one was polite, abstemious, austere, self-made; the other was gluttonous, bibulous, sybaritic, and born into privilege. Each believed in his military genius, artistic soul, and divine destiny as leader of his people. Each witnessed the end of the empire he'd worked his life to strengthen.

In contrast to Hitler's evil, Churchill's qualities glow bright and pure. Churchill was lucky to have been pitted against one so unambiguously wicked; had history instead paired him with Gandhi, for example, he'd be remembered differently.

In the view of history, despite the presence of other imposing figures—Roosevelt, Stalin, Mussolini, Eisenhower,

Montgomery, Chiang Kai-shek, de Gaulle, Tojo—it is the opposition of Churchill and Hitler that captures the essence of the Second World War.

Although Churchill claimed that he shared only one thing with Hitler—"a horror of whistling"—they shared many of the qualities that buttress a leader's power. Each had charisma, confidence, eloquence, physical stamina, and a high tolerance for risk. Each was ruthless, driven, obsessed with military power, fascinated by science, self-educated, self-absorbed, with a strong historical imagination. They'd both proved themselves in battle, and both had a surprising passion for painting. They both sought to control every aspect of the war, from grand strategy to minor details (Churchill worrying about soldiers' beer ration, Hitler considering what music should be used as radio fanfares to announce German victories).

Each leader had a deep faith in his destiny and in the destiny of his race. From his youth, Churchill believed himself fated to play a vital role in preserving the Empire and its traditions. He saw himself as a bulwark, the savior of something ancient and precious, the leader of a people who would once again triumph in defense of freedom. Hitler saw himself as a purifier and sole creator of something new. With the thousand-year Reich—which lasted twelve years, three months, and ten days—he wanted to destroy and transform, not preserve. Hitler's belief in his destiny was so profound that the near success of a 1944 assassination attempt actually comforted him; he believed his escape proved, once again, that Providence assured him victory. And after all, it's true that at the Reich's height, by diplomacy and war, Hitler— son of a minor official in rural Austria, a once-aimless drifter with little education—had achieved triumphs worthy of comparison to Napoleon.

But far more significant than similarities were differences—how Churchill and Hitler each used his capacity for leadership. Churchill, for all his fascination with modern technology and desire to shape the future, stood as the embodiment of time-honored standards and customs. Hitler instead wanted to force the future of Germany and the world. He was the product of past wrongs and grievances, and he ushered in a new order: modern, frighteningly efficient, employing "science" for mass destruction, systematic breeding, and racial purification. The Nazi swastika, the black eagle, the rallies lit by searchlight, were meant to whip individuals into an obedient, frenzied mass. There were no enduring principles to which Hitler adhered, no code to constrain his actions. He boasted:

> I am willing to sign anything. . . . I am prepared to guarantee all frontiers and to make non-aggression pacts and friendly alliances with anybody. . . . Why should I not make an agreement in good faith today and unhesitatingly break it tomorrow if the future of the German people demands it?

(Hitler's candor could give pause to revisionists who argue that Churchill should have found a way to secure peace with Hitler in 1940.)

Although both rallied their nations, it was Hitler who held his people in the tighter grip. Biographer Ian Kershaw noted that "few, if any, twentieth-century political leaders have enjoyed greater popularity among their own people than Hitler in the decade or so following his assumption of power on 30 January 1933." Churchill inspired respect and affection, but Hitler's effect was of a different magnitude. His relentless campaigning had given him a deep knowledge of the German people, and he divined the longings and resentments that festered below the surface of ordinary, respectable lives. Hitler had a profound grasp of the desires and weaknesses of others—other people and other nations—and he brilliantly exploited them. He saw, for example, how much Neville Chamberlain wanted peace, and he unhesitatingly played to that ambition.

One of the most characteristic differences between Churchill and Hitler was their attitude toward war and its consequences. Many considered Churchill a warmonger, but he wanted war to secure peace. In 1943, watching a film about the bombing of Germany—a policy he supported—he exclaimed, "Are we beasts? Are we taking this too far?" He was fueled by the desire not to destroy but to preserve. "I hate nobody except Hitler—and that is professional." On February 1, 1945, at the end of the bitter war, he wrote Clementine:

I am free to confess to you that my heart is saddened by the tales of the masses of German women and children flying along the roads everywhere in 40-mile long columns to the West before the advancing Armies. I am clearly convinced that they deserve it; but that does not remove it from one's gaze. The misery of the whole world appals me. . . .

Hitler never hesitated in his destruction. In 1939, he admonished, "Close your hearts to pity. Act brutally. Eighty million people must obtain what is their right. Their existence must be made secure. The stronger man is right." When he learned his personal bodyguard division had suffered heavy casualties, he cried, "Losses can never be too high! They sow the seeds of future greatness." Hitler deliberately harnessed the very worst in his people and encouraged the methodical expression of their most depraved impulses of extermination, torture, humiliation, and plunder.

A leader must have an instinctual grasp of the people. Some have argued that Churchill couldn't understand the struggles of ordinary Britons: he was a Duke's grandson and lived a life of valets and silver candlesticks and country houses. But while Churchill never waited in line for a bus, his imagination and his secure place in the world gave him sympathy for those whose troubles he didn't share. He visited the front when he could, toured bombed areas, and worried about the public's comforts and conveniences: he wrote countless memos about shortening the bus-stop lines, improving egg production, or making sure the troops got their medals. He insisted on the dignity of the common people and, for example, wrote General Ismay to insist that the term "Reserve Brigades" be used instead of "low-grade infantry brigades."

Churchill's faith in the British never flagged, and, confident of their courage, he never disguised the peril the country faced. On June 18, 1940, after France surrendered, Churchill addressed the House of Commons:

> The whole fury and might of the enemy must very soon be turned on us. Hitler knows that he will have to break us in this Island or lose the war. . . . [I]f we fail, then the whole world, including the United States . . . will sink into the abyss of a new Dark Age made more sinister, and perhaps more protracted, by the lights of perverted science. Let us therefore brace ourselves to our duties and so bear ourselves that if the British Empire and its Commonwealth last for a thousand years, men will still say, "This was their finest hour."

When someone told him that the best thing he'd done had been to give the people courage, he contradicted, "I never gave them courage; I was able to focus theirs."

Hitler was fueled by resentment and insecurity, both for himself and for Germany. Unlike Churchill, who thought nothing of being seen in his underwear or wrapped in a towel, Hitler had a morbid fear of looking ridiculous and even refused to be photographed wearing glasses. Although he claimed to act for Germany's benefit, at bottom, Hitler held the German people in contempt. Despite his advisers' pleas, Hitler almost never visited bombed cities or the front. When aides tried to show him pictures of the plight of German refugees, he pushed the photographs aside, saying at one point, "We can no longer afford to concern ourselves with the population." During the war's final years, Hitler refused to exploit his oratorical gifts to invigorate Germany. Goebbels urged Hitler to address the war-weary public. "A talk by the Fuhrer over the radio would be as good as a victorious battle today," Goebbels wrote in his diary on March 26, 1945. "In the hour of Britain's war crisis Churchill addressed himself to the nation in a magnificent speech and put it on its feet again. . . . Now that we are in a similar, though not much worse situation, we must do the same." Hitler knew his powers; why did he refuse to speak? Alan Bullock speculated, "Hitler's gifts as an orator had always depended on his flair for sensing what was in the minds of his audience. He no longer wanted to know what was in the minds of the German people; at all costs he must preserve his illusions." Hitler knew he wouldn't survive defeat, and he wanted Germany to perish with him. "If the war is to be lost, the nation also will perish. . . . There is no need to consider the basis even of a most primitive existence any longer. On the contrary it is better to destroy even that, and to destroy it ourselves. The nation has proved itself weak, and the future belongs to the stronger Eastern nation."

Historians battle over whether Hitler was a predictable outgrowth of German history or whether he was a monster utterly outside the ordinary. Hitler was both. He was the harvest of the fears, resentments, and yearnings of German history—but that doesn't mean that he was inevitable. And so with Churchill. The British experience simultaneously produced the fighter Churchill and the appeaser Chamberlain, whose policy also had logic, strategy, and good intentions behind it.

It was to Hitler that Churchill owed his enduring stature. Hitler didn't need Churchill, but Churchill wouldn't have been *Churchill* without Hitler. Churchill wrote many fine books, held many prominent offices, fought many battles both military and civilian. But it was his deep insight into Hitler and the Nazi regime, and his triumph in meeting that challenge, that immortalized Churchill. It's one of the ironies of history that the "wicked man" rescued Churchill from political exile and gave him the opportunity to rise to his great level. Hitler himself pointed this out: "But had this war not come, who would speak of Churchill?"

In May 1940, Churchill and Hitler faced off to the last. Alike and unalike, their opposition sums up that terrible age. Appropriately, for archetypes, both men lived in atmospheres suffused with symbols, portents, divine intervention. Consider just one historical echo: in ancient times, according to the Greek Herodotus, when King Croesus consulted the Delphic oracle about whether he should invade Persia, the oracle foretold that "*if Croesus attacked the Persians, he would destroy a mighty empire.*" Croesus attacked and lost; he returned to ask the oracle why it had answered falsely. The priestess explained, "After an answer like that, the wise thing would have been to send again to inquire which empire was meant." A nice twist; surely, the reader supposes, a clever invention of the priests or Herodotus. But then read Hitler's speech to the Reichstag on July 19, 1940, in which he predicts accurately:

> It almost causes me pain to think that I should have been selected by Fate to deal the final blow to the structure which these men [Churchill and his colleagues] have already set tottering. . . . *I shall speak a great prophecy. A great Empire will be destroyed, an Empire which it was never my intention to destroy.*

One modern theory holds that historical change is the result of material conditions and institutions, not the actions and ideas of outstanding individuals. Churchill and Hitler prove instead that a single person can change the course of history. Both were saved from death many times; the memory of these uncanny near misses—the bombs that exploded without reaching their targets, the bullets that didn't hit, the nearly fatal accidents and illnesses—provokes awe, with the thought of how different *it might have been.* Yet it also seems that history could not have been other than it was, with all its forces embodied in these two figures.

Hitler gives the Nazi salute.

Churchill flashes the V sign.

34

CHURCHILL EXPOSED

Missing Information Supplied

No biography can be complete or conclusive. The shelves groan with Churchill biographies, but what's the answer to the simple question, what was his birth weight? (Relevant to whether Churchill was premature when he was born, seven months after his parents married.) Even the longest account omits most facts about a subject's life, so it's the few chosen facts that give a portrait its shape.

Layers of fact pile higher and higher, and each additional fact may change the picture of the subject. A biographer's choice to highlight or dismiss certain episodes—controversial, offensive, or poignant— can vividly color a portrait. Readers unfamiliar with the subject's life are blind to the artful selection that's taking place.

This account of Churchill—like many, though not all—will conclude that Churchill was one of the greatest heroes of his time. But unlike a fictional hero who obediently performs an assigned role, Churchill muddied his identity with contradictions and shortcomings. Consider some unfortunate facts that, up to this point, have been passed over.

To shield his reputation, this account has downplayed Churchill's deplorable attitudes toward race. Churchill used opprobrious terms like *blackamoor, chink, wop,* and *baboo* and distinguished between the white race and others. For example, he wrote that at a September 1944 conference, he was "glad to record" that "the British Empire . . . was still keeping its position, with a total population, including the Dominions and Colonies, of only seventy million white people." He never outgrew his views. His doctor recalled that in 1955, Churchill asked whether "blacks got measles. . . . When he was told that there was a very high mortality among negroes from measles he growled: 'Well, there are plenty left. They've a high rate of production.' "

Churchill's disdain for women's company—except for a few beauties and a few brilliant conversationalists—has also been glossed over. His cousin Anita Leslie recalled, "Winston regarded males as the people who mattered; the ones who made the world go round. This did not mean that he was incapable of deep love for women, but what could women actually do except please and inspire the male sex?" Early on, Churchill had opposed votes for women: female suffrage was "contrary to natural law and the practice of civilized states"; women were "adequately represented by their husbands." Later, he supported, in theory, female suffrage. But militant suffragettes fired his opposition with their demands (he refused to be "henpecked on a question of such grave importance"), he thought there were already too many "ignorant voters," and he feared disturbance of the political equilibrium, and so his support was not passionate or even consistent.

As for the right to vote, contradicting his standing as democracy's great defender, as late as the 1930s, Churchill wrote newspaper articles advocating abandoning the "complete democracy" of one adult, one vote and returning to the traditional system that favored "more responsible elements." Wishing perhaps for the system that had been in place when he entered Parliament in 1900, when not even a third of Britons could vote, in 1930 he wrote with regret about earlier times when "we had a real political democracy led by a hierarchy of statesmen, and not a fluid mass distracted by newspapers . . . before the liquefaction of the British political system had set in."

This account has also ignored instances of brutality and vulgarity. For example, Churchill as Home Secretary advocated the forced sterilization of "mental degenerates" and, in a 1910 letter that reads as if drafted by a Nazi, argued, "The unnatural and increasingly rapid growth of the feeble-minded and insane classes . . . constitutes a national and race danger which it is impossible to exaggerate." Years later, a young Labour MP drove to Chartwell to apologize to Churchill after insulting him on the floor of the House. The MP arrived and gave Churchill's valet his name and purpose. Churchill was on the toilet; when his valet delivered the message, Churchill replied, "Tell him I'm on the privy and can take only one shit at a time."

Churchill never hesitated to use his wit to attack, and his cuts were all the harsher for being so memorable. In 1931,

criticizing Labour Prime Minister Ramsay MacDonald during a debate in the House of Commons, Churchill related:

> I remember when I was a child, being taken to the cele-
> brated Barnum's Circus which contained an exhibition of
> freaks and monstrosities, but the exhibit on the pro-
> gramme which I most desired to see was the one de-
> scribed as "The Boneless Wonder." My parents judged
> that that spectacle would be too revolting and demoralis-
> ing for my youthful eyes. I have waited fifty years to see
> the Boneless Wonder—sitting on the Treasury Bench.

When, returning from Munich in 1938, Prime Minister
Chamberlain waved the paper with Hitler's signature,
Churchill scoffed, "See that old town clerk looking at
European affairs through the wrong end of a municipal
drainpipe." He referred to U.S. Secretary of State John Foster
Dulles as "Dull, Duller, Dulles." Of Labour Prime Minister
Clement Attlee's modesty, Churchill said, "But then, he has
a great deal to be modest about."

Churchill is praised for his military innovations. What
about all his bad ideas? Just months before the Munich
Agreement, he criticized the Hurricane and Spitfire fighter
planes, which would save England in 1940. He was initially
convinced that armored ships were invincible against
bombers, unless a bomb dropped down the ship's funnel. He
received £100,000 to develop an earth-cutting machine
that came to nothing. He persisted in believing, contrary to
experience, that resistance movements inside occupied

countries could be highly effective. He ordered studies of gas and chemical warfare reprisals as well as a scheme for destroying, one by one, a hundred German towns.

Does including this suppressed material make the picture of Churchill more or less true? Both.

35

CHURCHILL TRUE OR FALSE

Challenged Assumptions

Facts have an irresistible glamor and authority, but they're slippery: the actual life of a public figure like Churchill becomes obscured by myth, by assumptions we make, and by facts we think we know. Pulling information out of context in a crude "True or False?" quiz highlights the difficulty of grasping the true facts of a life, even a life as familiar as Churchill's.

Circle "True" or "False." See end of chapter for answers.

1. **True / False**
   Churchill was a polo champion.
2. **True / False**
   Churchill was a fencing champion.
3. **True / False**
   Churchill owned a champion racehorse.
4. **True / False**
   As a youth, Churchill hounded his mother for money.

5. **True / False**

   As a youth, Churchill paid for his former nanny's funeral and the upkeep of her grave.

6. **True / False**

   At age twenty-seven, Churchill was one of the world's highest-paid newspaper reporters.

7. **True / False**

   Churchill was offered £10,000 to write a screenplay.

8. **True / False**

   When Churchill was captured by the Boers in 1899, it was General Louis Botha, leader of the Commandos and later South Africa's first Prime Minister, who took him prisoner.

9. **True / False**

   Churchill's mother married a man sixteen days older than her son.

10. **True / False**

    Churchill's mother married a man three years younger than her son.

11. **True / False**

    Churchill never attended a university.

12. **True / False**

    Churchill won the Nobel Prize in literature.

13. **True / False**

    Churchill didn't see *Hamlet* until he was in his late seventies.

14. **True / False**

    Churchill altered his war memoirs to avoid antagonizing President Eisenhower.

15. **True / False**

    Churchill was a Freemason.

16. **True / False**

    After being blackballed at an exclusive club, Churchill founded his own.

17. **True / False**

    Out of superstition, Churchill insisted that a champagne bottle be passed to the left around a table.

18. **True / False**

    Churchill had a daughter who died as a child.

19. **True / False**

    Churchill had a daughter who became a chorus girl.

20. **True / False**

    Churchill had a daughter who committed suicide.

21. **True / False**

    Churchill's great-granddaughter was one of Princess Diana's wedding attendants.

22. **True / False**

    Churchill's family nickname was "Pig."

23. **True / False**

    Clementine once threw a bowl of spinach at her husband's head.

24. **True / False**

    Clementine once wrote a Prime Minister to beg him to find Winston a place in the government.

25. **True / False**

    Clementine once sold a necklace to pay household expenses.

26. **True / False**

    When Clementine learned that Winston had been injured, she rushed to the hospital without putting on her shoes.

27. **True / False**

    When Churchill returned in 1939 as First Lord of the Admiralty, a message flashed out to all ships: "Winston is back."

28. **True / False**

    Churchill was dressed each day by a valet.

29. **True / False**

    Churchill wore pale pink silk underwear.

30. **True / False**

    Churchill was accused of homosexual misconduct.

31. **True / False**

    One of Churchill's closest associates was an effeminate aesthete.

32. **True / False**

    Churchill was rumored to have an illegitimate child.

33. **True / False**

    Churchill was accused of accepting a bribe.

34. **True / False**

    Churchill hated paper clips.

35. **True / False**

    Churchill demanded that the British civil service substitute "Yes" for "The answer is in the affirmative" in official communications.

36. **True / False**

    When reports indicated that Germany was preparing to

bomb Coventry, Churchill refused to jeopardize intelligence sources by sending aid.

37. **True / False**

Churchill supported the policy of bombing German civilians.

38. **True / False**

Churchill preferred white wine to red wine.

39. **True / False**

At a conference in Egypt, Churchill wanted Egyptians excluded from his hotel.

40. **True / False**

Churchill sent £2 each month for fifty years to a former Indian servant.

41. **True / False**

Churchill refused the offer of a dukedom.

42. **True / False**

As First Lord in 1940, Churchill traveled with a suicide pill in his pen in case of capture.

43. **True / False**

Churchill pioneered the concept and development of the tank.

44. **True / False**

Churchill pioneered the concept and development of floating landing harbors.

45. **True / False**

Churchill pioneered the establishment of the British Air Force.

46. **True / False**

Churchill worked to ensure that Air Force officers were drawn from the social elite.

47. **True / False**

Churchill once traveled on a holiday with eight hundred pounds of luggage.

48. **True / False**

Churchill was the savior of his country.

Churchill made the following statements:

49. **True / False**

"I have a keen aboriginal desire to kill several of these odious dervishes."

50. **True / False**

"I do not care so much for the principles I advocate as for the impression which my words produce and the reputation they give me."

51. **True / False**

"No one can travel even for a little while among the Kikuyu tribes without acquiring a liking for these light-hearted, tractable, if brutish children, or without feeling that they are capable of being instructed and raised from their present degradation."

52. **True / False**

"I only wish I were more worthy of you, and more able to meet the inner needs of your soul."

53. **True / False**

"We have got all we want in territory, and our claim to be left in the unmolested enjoyment of vast and splendid possessions, mainly acquired by violence, largely maintained by force, often seems less reasonable to others than to us."

54. **True / False**

Of the Navy: "Traditions! What traditions? Rum, sodomy—and the lash!"

55. **True / False**

"I know this war is smashing and shattering the lives of thousands every moment, and yet—I cannot help it—I enjoy every second I live."

56. **True / False**

"As to freedom of the press, why should any man be allowed to buy a printing press and disseminate pernicious opinions calculated to embarrass the government?"

57. **True / False**

"A universal suffrage electorate with a majority of women voters will have shown themselves incapable of preserving those forms of government under which our country has grown great."

58. **True / False**

"It is said that famous men are usually the product of an unhappy childhood."

59. **True / False**

"India is no more a political personality than Europe. India is a geographical term. It is no more a united nation than the Equator."

60. **True / False**

"Thus the world lives on hopes that the worst is over, and that we may yet live to see Hitler a gentler figure in a happier age."

61. **True / False**

"The greatest cross I have to bear is the Cross of Lorraine."

62. **True / False**

"Kindly remember I am Winston Churchill. Tell the station master to stop the train."

63. **True / False**

"We have now reached the dawn of what is called the sixteenth century, which means all the years in the hundred years that begin with fifteen."

Answers: All true, except for 8, 27, 36, 54, and 61. These well-known Churchill stories are apocryphal.

36

THE TRAGEDY OF WINSTON CHURCHILL, ENGLISHMAN

The Meaning of His Life

Within Churchill's ordinary human existence—an epigram thrown off during debate, a hernia operation, a whiskey before lunch—a spontaneous work of art reveals itself. For when we consider his life in literary, rather than human, terms, we see that it measures up to the strictest standards of composition, those required by tragedy. His biography is like a Greek drama made of facts literally true.

While it might seem that imposing the literary construction of tragedy on his life would obscure its truth, it is the devices of art that plunge the mind into reality. It is the presence of this hidden, formal beauty diffused through the record of facts that distinguishes Churchill's life from the lives of other great figures; it gives his story a fatefulness, and a transcendent power, almost never found in real life.

Pliny wrote, "Of all the blessings given to man by nature none is greater than a timely death." Had Churchill died at the end of the war, he'd have died a hero. He'd been voted out of office, but no one denied that he'd played a matchless part. The world loaded him with honors and adulation.

But for two long decades after the war, he watched as the Empire dwindled, as Britain turned Socialist, as the Soviets dropped their iron curtain across Europe. This long anti-climax crowned Churchill as another kind of hero—a *tragic hero,* who enacted, in his individual life, a tragic drama of such pure and perfect construction as to stagger belief in its reality. He wasn't the kind of tragic hero who appears in newspaper headlines (MAILMAN DIES IN TRAGIC FIRE) but one who meets the rigorous formal test of the most exacting, and traditionally the most exalted, of all literary forms: *tragedy.*

After twenty-five hundred years, tragedy remains clouded in mystery. What, precisely, are its elements? Why does tragedy exhilarate us with the spectacle of suffering? Is modern tragedy possible? And how could Winston Churchill, in his actual, day-to-day life, personify a tragedy?

In its essentials, tragedy demands a hero who commands our attention and goodwill. Usually, though not necessarily, this figure has high rank and intellectual depth. A tragic hero comes into his fate at a time of change—in a melancholy twilight when one world is dying (and with it, the old ways and values) and another, rising.

The hero is brought to disaster by some *hamartia* ("error," "flaw"), a willful pride or obsession that brings about his downfall. Often, this flaw takes the form of *hubris* ("inso-lence," "pride"). The hero's hubris deceives him; knowing

himself to be strong, he believes he can overcome any ob-
stacle and hurtles himself toward destruction. In his over-
weening commitment to a single purpose, he fails to
understand the true relationship between himself and . . .
what? The gods, fortune, destiny, necessity, binding obligation, inevitability, history, eternal nature, laws beyond
human understanding. And yet, despite this flaw, a tragic
hero exhibits a greatness of spirit, a force or sensitivity or
representativeness, that enthralls us.

The tragic hero is driven, with an uncompromising will,
to achieve an urgent and significant purpose. The actions
taken in fulfillment of that purpose—and this is tragedy's
fearsome crux—*necessarily* and *inevitably* condemn the hero
to suffer. Here is the formal perfection of tragedy: doom
waits from the first moments of the hero's struggle, and the
consummation of his purpose fulfills his pitiful destiny. King
Lear demands to learn how much his daughters love him . . .
and he does.

The tragic hero's high position and power heighten the
pity and fear roused by his downfall; his worldly and spiritual
powers allow him to fight more tenaciously and, in defeat, to
suffer more deeply. Tragedy is larger than life, to rouse our
emotions.

Rarely does actual life attain the clarity and inevitability of
literature—especially that of tragedy, a form that exists on the
high plane of symbol and archetype. Churchill's life does.

Churchill exactly embodies the traditional tragic hero:
aristocratic, eloquent, and in high office not by inheritance but by having seized supreme powers. His language

was princely and his tears, noble, because commonplaces wouldn't express his passions. He lived his life not in private but in public, a commander destined to rule others. He overflowed with energy: a statesman and writer, and also war hero, painter, polo champion, pilot, bricklayer, the head of a family. He was a son searching for his lost father. In his world and time, he knew everyone and was part of everything that happened. Isaiah Berlin described him: "A man larger than life, composed of bigger and simpler elements than ordinary men, a gigantic historical figure during his own lifetime, superhumanly bold, strong, and imaginative . . . a mythical hero who belongs to a legend as much to reality, the largest human being of our time." And yet his cigars and champagne, his five children and his debts, remind us of his bonds to the physical, the earthly, the actual; he is greater than us, but one of us.

He compromised with no one in his pursuit of his goal: the advancement of England. Whatever he did, he did for England. *Naught shall make us rue, If England to itself do rest but true.* "His spirit is indomitable," noted an associate in 1940, "and even if France and England should be lost, I feel he would carry on the crusade himself with a band of privateers." Like every tragic figure, Churchill was true to his fault; he held back nothing and refused to surrender. He recognized this quality in himself. In his one novel, Churchill described the character Savrola, his double: "The life he lived was the only one he could ever live; he must go on to the end."

As if his story were written for the stage, there was a precise moment, on June 4, 1940, when Churchill called down his tragic destiny: *"We shall defend our Island, whatever the cost may be."* It's this pronouncement that hurls Churchill into the ranks of tragic heroes. It was then, at the dizzying apex, that his fortune began its inexorable descent. He couldn't see this, but we can.

The trap was perfect. (Consider Oedipus or Macbeth, for whom similar traps were laid by prophecy.) Churchill swore to preserve the Empire he loved—*we shall go on to the end,* he promised; *we shall never surrender, whatever the cost may be*— and in saving it, he set it speeding toward its demise. The vast expense of the war, as well as the social forces it accelerated, caused Britain to relinquish its supreme position. But had Churchill foreseen that outcome, what would he have done differently? He had to choose and couldn't choose well. If he'd made a bargain with Hitler, the Empire he loved wouldn't have survived. All Europe would have been crushed beneath the Nazi boot and Britain reduced to a German satellite—if that. Even if he'd known the cost of his victory, he would never have made a compromise peace with Hitler, or withdrawn from the war once the United States and Soviet Russia had joined, or husbanded resources from the fight to safeguard the Empire's position after the war. Instead, under Churchill, Britain impoverished itself by spending massively to defend its Empire in the Middle East and Far East—the very Empire Britain would relinquish soon after the war's end.

Churchill was lionized as the only man who could have uni-fied England against Hitler, the only man who could have led the fight to victory; and therefore, he made himself the chief architect of the Empire's undoing. That is the tragic paradox: the hero gets what he wanted, but at a price he never imagined, and he could make no better choice. Churchill's climactic moment—*In all our long history we have never seen a greater day than this*—contained the turn of the wheel. He would survive to fight helplessly the consequence of the events he himself had put in motion.

His bitter destiny attended his very nature and his first hopeful actions. "*In great or small station, in Cabinet or in the firing line, alive or dead, my policy is, 'Fight on.'* " What was he fighting for? "I have always faithfully served two public causes which, I think, stand supreme—the maintenance of the enduring greatness of Britain and her Empire, and the historical continuity of our Island life."

Churchill lost his struggle. "We answered all the tests," he said. "But it was useless." A few years before he died, he told his daughters, "I have achieved much to achieve nothing in the end." He confided, "In the end it has all been for nothing. . . . The Empire *I* believed in has gone." Perhaps the reason he lost the 1945 election is that the British people perceived his relentless will and knew that he was still fighting to save something they knew was already lost, something they didn't wish to keep.

The fact of Churchill's tragedy doesn't mean it was regrettable that his Empire fell, but even the onlooker who rejoices at its end feels the passion of Churchill's resolution. The tragedy inheres in his struggle and pain, not in the merit of the object for which he suffered. Would we say to

Antigone, Why throw your life away for your dead brother? Would we say to Ahab, Stop hunting the whale and save yourself? We accept the hero's world and, with it, the hero's purpose.

Churchill chose his course. He suffered a defeat within his victory, but that defeat was also a sublime fulfillment. The Empire he believed in had gone. But still, good had won over evil.

Generally, a tragedy's resolution makes us feel that the hero's suffering has restored the world's disturbed order. Tragedy sends us away comforted; somehow, despite the frightening tumult of our existence, we feel that "life is at bottom indestructibly joyous and powerful," as Nietzsche described it. This, the stark tragedy of Winston Churchill accomplishes. The very familiarity of his story—with its spectacular rises and falls—deepens the satisfaction it gives; no shock of actual surprise distracts us from the tragic spectacle.

Churchill's tragedy exalts us, too, because of the nature of his enemy. No tyrant—though he may have killed, enslaved, or tortured as many or more—horrifies us as Hitler does. Germany had been democratic, highly educated, cultured, prosperous, and ruled by law, and it was Hitler who led the German people's descent into barbarism. Having risen higher, they fell further. Churchill opposed this threat from its earliest moments. He, and perhaps only he, rose to the level of events. He pledged everything to the fight, and in the end, he gave everything.

As befits a tragic hero, his tragedy was not private—it was

endured in public and engaged a nation. On one hand is the spectacle of a great people, led by their champion, fighting for freedom, until the end. On the other is the immense vision of a mighty Empire sinking: of course it's true—it *must* be true—that one of Churchill's greatest influences was Gibbon's *The Decline and Fall of the Roman Empire*.

The essence of tragedy is not sorrow but solemnity: the remorseless progress of the world. That which bore Churchill up, crashed him down. Having pledged to defend the glory of England *at all costs,* he must pay the heavy price: the end of the Empire he was so determined to preserve. Having chosen to resist the Empire's destruction, he must feel its loss more profoundly than anyone else. Having managed to seize power yet again at the end of his long career, he must confront the brutal reality that his world had vanished beyond his ability to restore it. Having been given the gift of great vitality, he must bear long life and the knowledge it brought.

37

CHURCHILL IN PORTRAIT

A Likeness

Recognizing they're at the mercy of their portraitists, most leaders keep images of themselves under the strictest control possible. Like Alexander the Great, who permitted only a few trusted artists to depict him, and John Kennedy, who surrounded himself with admiring writers, Churchill recognized that a portrait could illuminate his character in dangerous ways.

In a painted portrait, the full weight of a personality can be seen, with an extra dimension not captured in a photograph. This wild element worried Churchill, who aimed to control his image in history. He was painted many times, but the portrait that reveals most about Churchill is the portrait he hated.

In a unique honor, for Churchill's eightieth birthday, both Houses of Parliament presented him with a portrait of himself painted by Graham Sutherland, one of the finest contemporary artists. Because Parliament commissioned the birthday portrait, Churchill had no control over the choice of artist or the painting.

At first, all had gone well with the gift. Churchill and Clementine liked Sutherland and his wife, and Churchill enjoyed the sittings. With his love for pomp, uniform, and tradition, he'd wanted to be portrayed wearing his robes of the Garter, but Sutherland insisted that Churchill forgo the resplendent blue velvet mantle and the velvet hat with its sweeping ostrich plume to wear his working-day black coat and bow tie instead.

When Churchill saw the completed portrait, he felt betrayed; Sutherland had depicted him as a "gross & cruel monster." Churchill loathed the picture so much he considered declining to accept it. In the end, he didn't refuse the painting, but at the presentation ceremony, he didn't say he liked it, either. "The portrait is a remarkable example of *modern art,*" he said with obvious irony to the audience, which erupted in laughter and sympathetic applause. "It certainly combines force and candour." Privately, he called it "filthy" and "malignant" and said it made him look like "a drinking sot."

Photographs from the presentation ceremony emphasize the contrast between the living Churchill and the Churchill portrait. Standing on the dais, the eighty-year-old Churchill appears filled with energy and humor. He gestures energetically and sets the crowd laughing. Behind him, on display, is a different Churchill. No smile, no cigar, no noble determination: he appears not as a dashing war hero or serene statesman but as an old, stubborn man, weighed down by mortal bulk, with a bald head, fleshy nose, and mouth turned down at the corners. The portrait doesn't hint at Churchill's famous wit or magnanimity but reveals all his grim determination, pride, and frustration. Churchill sits braced against some on-slaught, wearily ready as always to fight again. He looks heavy and yet somehow strangely insubstantial, at least in re-production—and that's the only way to see the portrait now.

The portrait no longer exists. Clementine secretly de-stroyed it sometime in 1955 or 1956. Churchill's hatred of the picture, and his resentment at how he'd been portrayed, preyed on his mind so much that Clementine promised him it would never be seen again.

Was it the portrait's untruth, or its truth, that caused Churchill so much anguish? Around the same time he re-ceived it, just before his final resignation as Prime Minister, he said of himself, "I feel like an aeroplane at the end of its flight, in the dusk, with petrol running out, in search of a safe landing." Sutherland had seen this, too.

Churchill, portrayed by Graham Sutherland.

Churchill and his portrait, photographed during the eightieth-birthday celebration.

38

CHURCHILL'S LAST DAYS
How He Died

How a great figure like Churchill died is one of the most interesting facts of his life. Few choose when or how they die, yet death, however it comes, always seems somehow characteristic; though involuntary, it makes a dramatic flourish that influences our interpretation of the life. Joan of Arc's martyrdom, Napoleon's captivity, Lincoln's assassination, Oscar Wilde's exile—different deaths would have changed the emphasis of their lives. The story of Churchill, his life and significance, would have been different had he died by an assassin's bullet, on the battlefield, or in a plane crash. Instead, he died quietly in his bed, in 1965.

No one more than Churchill would have wanted to write his own death—a hero's death, at the height of his powers. Of Roosevelt, who died just before victory, Churchill said, "He died in harness. . . . What an enviable death was his!" In a 1945 letter, General Sir Alan Brooke observed that Churchill seemed determined to risk his life, and certainly a wartime death would have satisfied Churchill's love for the bold and dramatic. Clementine believed the war would finish off both of them. "I never think of after the war," Clementine said in 1944. "I think Winston will die when it's over. . . . You see, he's seventy and I'm sixty and we're putting all we have into this war, and it will take all we have." Instead, Churchill lived on for two decades.

Ambition had always fueled his terrific energy, and he fought on to achieve a second stint as Prime Minister, after his loss in 1945. After his retirement in 1955, however, his characteristic vitality dropped. Churchill once observed that "the wielding of power keeps men young," and when he stepped down from office for the last time, he became slower, more deaf, without focus. He spent hours listening to recordings of his speeches on a portable record player. As in a fairy tale, one of Fortune's greatest gifts to Churchill—his indestructibility—twisted itself into an affliction. "Blessings become curses," he said to his doctor. "You kept me alive and now . . ." Churchill hung on in Parliament until 1964, aged eighty-nine, but by then, he'd sunk into the melancholy of old age. "I've got to kill time till time kills me." He said to his daughter Diana, "My life is over, but it is not yet ended."

Churchill finally died on January 24, 1965, at age ninety. The date is significant. Jock Colville recalled a remark Churchill made one morning in the early 1950s: "Today is the twenty-fourth of January. It is the day my father died. It is the day that I shall die too." And in fact, after his final stroke, Churchill lay unconscious for many days until he died on January 24, seventy years to the day of his father's death.

His last words were, "I'm so bored with it all."

His death came as a shock to his countrymen. For most of them, Churchill had been a presence—a name in the newspaper, a caricature in the cartoons, a voice on the radio, a face on the screen—for their entire lives. After all, he'd thrust himself into the public eye in 1898, with his first book, and had become a national hero in 1899, when he escaped from the Boer military prison.

And Churchill? Did a pageant of memories console him as he lingered on those last silent days, to die on the day he'd chosen, the same day as his father had died? Perhaps his life slid backward from the present day, with its iron curtain and hydrogen bombs; back from his finest hour, the Second World War; and back from the First World War and the horror of the Dardanelles, and from his daring escape from the Boers, and the dash and glamor of the Indian campaigns; back, back, to his lovely mother, like the Evening Star with diamonds in her hair, and to his disdainful father, whom he admired so much; back to Nanny Everest and his earliest memory, the sight of scarlet soldiers on horseback. And through it all was his Island, the precious stone set in the silver sea. He might have remembered all this and more as he waited for his appointed hour.

It was all finished now. Throughout his career, responsible people agreed that Churchill, for all his brilliance, lacked judgment. He thrust himself forward, he interfered, he was mistrusted, feared, disliked.

But Churchill had his sights fixed on history. He strove to earn his place there. His greatest dread was being shut out of responsible position, unable to direct the course of events. Asked what year of his life he'd choose to relive, he instantly replied, "Nineteen-forty every time, every time."

When Churchill died, flags flew at half-mast all over the country. Big Ben was silenced. His body lay in state in Westminster Hall for three days, and despite the bitter cold, hundreds of thousands of people filed past the coffin. Television networks all over the world broadcast the procession and service. By tradition, the monarch attends only funerals of members of the royal family, but Queen Elizabeth broke with precedent and attended the funeral. Actor Laurence Olivier read from the great speeches. Reflecting Churchill's love for military pomp, the funeral featured multigun salutes, an RAF fly-past, and the playing of "Rule, Britannia."

Churchill's body was taken up the Thames and then by train to Oxfordshire, then buried in the Bladon village churchyard, near Blenheim Palace. He had planned to be buried at his beloved Chartwell, but changed his mind in 1959: he wanted to be buried alongside his father. This ceremony was simple, with only two wreaths: "To my Darling Winston, Clemmie" and "From the Nation and Commonwealth. In grateful remembrance. Elizabeth R."

In Westminster Abbey rests a marble tablet inscribed "Remember Winston Churchill."

39

My Churchill

Judgment

Every biography raises questions of judgment, because without judgment, the life lacks significance.

Now you must arrive at your own verdict, must decide how to balance faults against virtues and successes against failures, what to pardon because of changing standards, how much to be swayed by sentiment, how to weigh the evidence. The facts mount up, but what is true?

Here is my *Churchill. Others look at this history and see a different "Churchill," but this is mine. It's a bold and simple view, which is, after all, how he saw the world himself and how he sought to be remembered.*

Now time's lens pulls back to reveal more of the whole, less detail. Only the most significant people and events remain visible; small incidents blur and vanish. My Churchill comes into view—not in shades of gray, only brilliant colors—embodying a few bright themes. His noble tragedy is part of history now.

It's a relief to consider Churchill, so true, so bold, with his heroic values, his exaltation of raw ambition into his country's larger good, his immense energy and insight. His certainty and grandiosity—even his whiskey and cigars—light up our modest age. He held to a single conviction: *Naught shall make us rue, If England to itself do rest but true.* What was the source of his greatness? Not his predictions or his strategies, but his determination to fight on, whatever the cost, for everything that mattered most.

He pushed his way through the changes that engulfed his Victorian world. There he was, the fighting spirit of Britain: the grandson of a Duke, a mongrel half-American, a self-advertiser, a drinker, an imperialist, in debt—dressed in his siren suit and waving a cigar. He cried, he sang, he called Hitler "that Bad Man," he decorated his signature with drawings of pigs. He had nothing to explain or excuse. He didn't pretend to pay attention to other people, or accommodate himself to popular positions, or even trouble about his own dignity. He imagined himself the romantic hero in the Island story—and it was true, he *was* that hero.

The time-bound Churchill possessed contradictions and faults that diminished him; his tremendous virtues were tainted by his flaws. He did not rise above many of the limitations of his age or his character. But let that history fall away now. Time passes, and although his faults aren't forgotten, from our distant vantage point, we can remember Churchill as he wanted to be remembered.

At the end, he believed his struggles had failed: "The Empire *I* believed in has gone." But had he lived longer, he would have seen that *he'd won after all*. He hoped to see a world led by English-speaking people, united by the English language, fighting for English ideals. All this has happened. The Island story he loved has changed, but not ended.

Now *my* Churchill can emerge, more forceful, more true, than that other Churchill, who lived and died. He's taken his place in the finest hour of the glorious history he imagined—a history of an ancient race, thatched cottages, noble battles, and a father who loved him.

There he is, my Churchill, braced on the quarterdeck of HMS *Prince of Wales,* cigar in his hand, surrounded by British and American sailors. For the moment, the urgencies of war have quieted the restlessness and ambition that dog him. His powers, too strenuous for peacetime, at last suit the hour.

Now he addresses the troops. *"We shall go on to the end,"* he promises; *"we shall never surrender."* Flags snap in the breeze, and Roosevelt's wheelchair creaks its way across the deck, and Churchill leads everyone, Britons and Americans together, in singing. In all his long history he will never see a greater day than this. Tears are running down his cheeks, tears not of sorrow but of wonder and admiration.

This isn't everyone's Churchill, but it's my Churchill.

It all happened long ago and far away, but I can see Winston Churchill more clearly than I can see the page on which I write.

40

Remember Winston Churchill

Epitaph

It is all true, or it ought to be; and more and better besides. And wherever men are fighting against barbarism, tyranny, and massacre, for freedom, law, and honour, let them remember that the fame of their deeds, even though they themselves be exterminated, may perhaps be celebrated as long as the world rolls round.

—Winston Churchill, *A History of the English-Speaking Peoples*

NOTES

Introduction

Page

1 *Prime Minister Churchill . . . Russia."* Doris Kearns Goodwin, *No Ordinary Time: Franklin and Eleanor Roosevelt: The Home Front in World War II* (New York: Simon and Schuster, 1994), 254–55.

1 *"this was their finest hour,"* David Cannadine, ed., *Blood, Toil, Tears, and Sweat: The Speeches of Winston Churchill* (Boston: Houghton Mifflin Company, 1989), 178.

2 *"The senior officers . . . discussion."* Winston Churchill, *My Early Life* (New York: Charles Scribner's Sons, 1930), 144.

2 *The expressions "Medal-hunter" . . . footsteps.* Ibid., 162.

3 *"Events were soon . . . afterwards."* Ibid., 372.

4 *"Churchill, unlike Hitler . . . eyes."* John Lukacs, *The Duel: Hitler vs. Churchill: 10 May–31 July 1940* (London: Phoenix Press, 1990), 7.

4 *"he could have filled buckets"* Harold Nicolson, *Diaries and Letters,* vol. 2, *The War Years, 1939–1945,* ed. Nigel Nicolson (New York: Atheneum, 1967), November 14, 1944.

4 *"Dark, vivacious, and magnificent . . . position."* William Manchester, *The Last Lion: Winston Spencer Churchill: Visions of Glory, 1874–1932* (Boston: Little, Brown and Company, 1983), 100.

5 *"Your trouble . . . much.* Lord Moran, *Churchill: Taken from the Diaries of Lord Moran* (Boston: Houghton Mifflin Company, 1966), 180. Diary entry of August 14, 1944; footnote omitted.

5   *We shall go on . . . nonsense."*   John Charmley, *Churchill: The End of Glory* (New York: Harcourt, Brace and Company, 1993), 411.

7   *"There's nothing much . . . unploughed."*   Virginia Cowles, *Winston Churchill: The Era and the Man* (New York: Harper & Brothers, 1953), vii.

7   *"These facts are . . . change."*   Virginia Woolf, *Collected Essays,* vol. 4 (New York: Harcourt, Brace & World, 1953), "The Art of Biography," 226.

9   *"The lay reader . . . equanimity."*   Janet Malcolm, *The Silent Woman: Sylvia Plath and Ted Hughes* (New York: Vintage, 1993), 175.

9   *"Another bloody monkey mind! . . . shut up."*   Paula R. Backscheider, *Reflections on Biography* (Oxford: Oxford University Press, 2001), 90.

10   *"This book does not . . . view."*   Winston Churchill, *A History of the English-Speaking Peoples,* vol. 1, *The Birth of Britain* (New York: Dodd, Mead and Company, 1956), viii.

1: Churchill as Liberty's Champion

17   *"There was a . . . end."*   Winston Churchill, *The Second World War,* vol. 2, *Their Finest Hour* (New York: Houghton Mifflin Company, 1949), 100.

17   *"Let us therefore . . . hour.'"*   David Cannadine, ed., *Blood, Toil, Tears, and Sweat: The Speeches of Winston Churchill* (Boston: Houghton Mifflin Company, 1989), 177–78.

17   *"In all our . . . this."*   Winston Churchill, *War Speeches,* vol. 5, *Victory* (Boston: Little, Brown and Company, 1946), 167.

18   *"The Englishman will not . . . are."*   Winston Churchill, *My Early Life: A Roving Commission* (New York: Charles Scribner's Sons, 1930), 221.

18   *"From Stettin in the Baltic . . . Continent."*   Geoffrey Best, *Churchill: A Study in Greatness* (New York: Hambledon and London, 2001), 278.

18   *"I want to die in England."*   Martin Gilbert, *Churchill: A Life* (New York: Henry Holt and Company, 1991), 957.

19   *"We shall fight . . . surrender."*   Churchill, *Their Finest Hour,* 118.

2: Churchill as Failed Statesman

20 *such as those by . . . colleague.* Several of Churchill's colleagues underwent name changes as a result of receiving titles; they are referred to throughout by the name most likely to be familar to readers. Thus, the Chief of the Imperial General Staff is called "General Sir Alan Brooke" in the text, though his diary, reflecting the title he was later given, is published under the name "Lord Alanbrooke."

22 *Winston was born . . . that.* William Manchester, *The Last Lion: Winston Spencer Churchill: Visions of Glory, 1874–1932* (Boston: Little, Brown and Company, 1983), 108.

22 *"It is very unkind . . . term."* Randolph S. Churchill, *Winston S. Churchill,* companion vol. 1, part 1 (Boston: Houghton Mifflin Company, 1967), 88.

23 *"This kind of war . . . game."* Winston Churchill, *My Early Life: A Roving Commission* (New York: Charles Scribner's Sons, 1930), 180.

25 *"He was hated . . . feared"* Lord Beaverbrook, *Politicians and the War* (Garden City: Doubleday, Doran and Company, 1959), 17.

25 *"Your first duty . . . Duke."* Consuelo Balsan, *The Glitter and the Gold* (Maidstone: George Mann Books, 1953), 57.

25 *His speeches were . . . extemporizing.* William Manchester, *The Last Lion: William Spencer Churchill: Alone, 1932–1940* (Boston: Little, Brown and Company, 1988), 34.

25 *"What's the use . . . seat?"* Manchester, *Visions of Glory,* 394.

26 *As Secretary of State . . . spending.* Basil Liddell Hart, "The Military Strategist," in *Churchill Revised: A Critical Assessment,* by A.J.P. Taylor et al. (New York: Dial Press, 1969), 200–201.

28 *"Churchill on the top . . . made."* Beaverbrook, *Politicians and the War,* 284.

28 *"temperamental like a film star . . . child."* Lord Alanbrooke, *War Diaries: 1939–1945,* eds. Alex Danchev and Daniel Todman (Berkeley: University of California Press, 2001), 450. Diary entry of August 30, 1943.

28 *Ordinary Britons were grateful . . . consumption.* John Keegan, *The Mask of Command* (New York: Penguin Books, 1987), 274.

28 *At a time when . . . brim.* John Pearson, *The Private Lives of Winston Churchill* (New York: Simon and Schuster, 1991), 283.

29 *At one meeting . . . of it."* Alger Hiss, *Recollections of a Life* (New York: Henry Holt and Company, 1988), 124. At Yalta, to Secretary of State Edward Stettinius.

29 *"is virtually dictator . . . servant."* Brian Gardner, *Churchill in Power: As Seen by His Contemporaries* (Boston: Houghton Mifflin Company, 1970), 213, quoting Admiral W. M. James, February 4, 1943.

31 *Even Clementine considered . . . Churchill.* Mary Soames, *Clementine Churchill: The Biography of a Marriage* (Boston: Houghton Mifflin Company, 1979), 63.

32 *in fact, one club's constitution . . . membership."* Manchester, *Alone,* 254.

32 *"Churchill stood for . . . victory."* John Charmley, *Churchill: The End of Glory* (New York: Harcourt, Brace and Company, 1993), 649.

4: Churchill's Finest Hour: May 28, 1940

38 *In the days before . . . independence.* John Lukacs, *Five Days in London: May 1940* (New Haven: Yale University Press, 1999), 117.

38 *His aim was . . . rot."* Earl of Birkenhead, *Halifax: The Life of Lord Halifax* (Boston: Houghton Mifflin Company, 1966), 458, quoting Halifax diary of May 27, 1940.

39 *"Nations which went down . . . finished."* Raymond Callahan, *Churchill: Retreat from Empire* (Wilmington: Scholarly Resources, 1984), 6.

39 *"quite casually . . . fight on.' "* Winston Churchill, *The Second World War*, vol. 2, *Their Finest Hour* (Boston: Houghton Mifflin Company, 1949), 100.

39 *I am convinced . . . ground.* Martin Gilbert, *Churchill: A Life* (New York: Henry Holt and Company, 1991), 651.

40 *In these dark days . . . Cause.* Churchill, *Their Finest Hour,* 91–92.

41 *Even though large . . . the Old.*   Ibid., 118.

41 *"You can always . . . you"*   Ibid., 279.

5: Churchill as Leader

42 *"would read a long . . . issue."*   John Colville, *The Fringes of Power: 10 Downing Street Diaries, 1939–1955* (New York: W. W. Norton & Company, 1985), 126.

43 *"Lots of people . . . plans."*   Winston Churchill, *War Speeches*, vol. 3, *Onward to Victory* (Boston: Little, Brown and Company, 1944), 126.

43 *"You ask, what is . . . victory."*   Roy Jenkins, *Churchill* (New York: Farrar, Straus and Giroux, 2001), 591.

43 *"rarely failed to inject . . . emotion."*   Dwight D. Eisenhower, "Churchill as an Ally in War," in *Churchill by His Contemporaries,* ed. Charles Eade (London: Reprint Society, 1953), 132.

44 *"Winston was never good . . . them."*   Lord Alanbrooke, *War Diaries: 1939–1945,* eds. Alex Danchev and Daniel Todman (Berkeley: University of California Press, 2001), 214. Note accompanying December 23, 1941.

44 *He found time . . . Tirpitz.*   Winston Churchill, *The Second World War,* vol. 4, *The Hinge of Fate* (Boston: Houghton Mifflin Company, 1950), 844.

45 *"His abdication . . . for us."*   Albert Speer, *Inside the Third Reich,* trans. Richard and Clara Winston (New York: Touchstone, 1970), 72.

45 *and in fact . . . salute.* Frances Lonsdale Donaldson, *Edward VIII* (Philadelphia: Lippincott & Company, 1974), 354.

6: Churchill's Genius with Words

47 *whether in his own . . . else*   For a thorough examination of the controversy regarding the use of an actor, Norman Shelley, to mimic Churchill's voice for broadcast of some speeches, see the essay by D. J. Wenden, "Churchill, Radio, and Cinema," in *Churchill: A Major New Assessment of His Life in Peace and War,* eds. Robert Blake and William Roger Louis (New York: W. W. Norton & Company, 1993), 236, appendix.

48 *"The ideas set forth . . . stake."* Winston Churchill, *The Second World War*, vol. 2, *Their Finest Hour* (Boston: Houghton Mifflin Company, 1949), 262.

48 *Sir, . . . polite."* Winston Churchill, *The Second World War*, vol. 3, *The Grand Alliance* (Boston: Houghton Mifflin Company, 1950), 610–11.

49 *" 'Sharks' for short," he added.* Winston Churchill, *The Second World War*, vol. 4, *The Hinge of Fate* (Boston: Houghton Mifflin Company, 1950), 956.

50 *"I don't think . . . better."* Churchill, *Their Finest Hour*, 166.

50 *"There I sat . . . home."* Essay by John Colville, in *Action This Day: Working with Churchill*, ed. John Wheeler-Bennett (New York: St. Martin's Press, 1969), 96, n. 1.

51 *"I cannot help feeling . . . leak out."* Peter Fleming, *Operation Sea Lion: The Projected Invasion of England in 1940* (New York: Akadine Press, 1956), 97.

51 *"First, it is . . . absence."* Robert Rhodes James, *Churchill: A Study in Failure* (New York: World Publishing Company, 1970), 33. Speech in the House of Commons, August 7, 1911.

51 *"I said . . . ashore."* Churchill, *Their Finest Hour*, 155.

51 *"Be on your guard . . . Britain."* Kay Halle, *Irrepressible Churchill* (New York: World Publishing Company, 1966), 163.

51 *"I have often made . . . days."* Martin Gilbert, *Churchill: A Life* (New York: Henry Holt and Company, 1991), 954.

52 *"Over 75 and below . . . Englishman!"* Halle, *Irrepressible Churchill*, 167.

52 *"In all our . . . than this."* Winston Churchill, *War Speeches*, vol. 5, *Victory* (Boston: Little, Brown and Company, 1946), 167.

52 *"It was a nation . . . roar."* Winston Churchill, *Winston S. Churchill: His Complete Speeches 1897–1963*, vol. 8, ed. Robert Rhodes James (New York: Chelsea House Publishers, 1974), 8608.

52 *"His great speeches . . . inarticulately."* Essay by Sir Ian Jacob, in *Action This Day: Working with Churchill*, ed. John Wheeler-Bennett (New York: St. Martin's Press, 1969), 182.

53 *"If this long island . . . ground."*   Martin Gilbert, *Churchill: A Life* (New York: Henry Holt and Company, 1991), 651.

53 *"Halifax's virtues . . . people.")*   Lord Moran, *Churchill: Taken from the Diaries of Lord Moran* (Boston: Houghton Mifflin Company, 1966), 347. Diary entry of December 7, 1947.

53 *"The stronger man is right,"*   Ian Kershaw, *Hitler, 1939–1945: Nemesis* (New York: W. W. Norton & Company, 2000), 209.

53 *"We shall never surrender."*   Churchill, *Their Finest Hour,* 118.

7: Churchill's Eloquence

62 *These cruel, wanton . . . removed.*   Winston Churchill, *Winston S. Churchill: His Complete Speeches 1897–1963*, vol. 6, ed. Robert Rhodes James (New York: Chelsea House Publishers, 1974), 6276–77.

63 *It fell to Neville Chamberlain . . . tomb?*   Winston Churchill, *War Speeches,* vol. 1, *The Unrelenting Struggle* (Boston: Little, Brown and Company, 1942), 4–5.

64 *The Nazi régime . . . aid.*   Ibid., 171, 173.

65 *No American will think . . . powder.*   Winston Churchill, *The Second World War,* vol. 3, *The Grand Alliance* (Boston: Houghton Mifflin Company, 1950), 607.

8: Churchill in Symbols

69 *"One of the most necessary . . . recognize."*   Winston Churchill, *Amid These Storms* (New York: Charles Scribner's Sons, 1932), 34.

71 *The V sign was . . . yours!"*   Paul Fussell, *Wartime: Understanding and Behavior in the Second World War* (New York: Oxford University Press, 1989), 149–50.

71 *"Perhaps such foibles . . . genius."*   Leslie Hore-Belisha, "How Churchill Influences and Persuades," in *Churchill by His Contemporaries,* ed. Charles Eade (London: Reprint Society, 1953), 271.

72 *"Winston dresses night and day . . . bricks."*   Diana Cooper, *Trumpets from the Steep* (Boston: Houghton Mifflin Company, 1960), 158.

72 *"already acquiring a definitely . . . than ever."* H. V. Morton, *Atlantic Meeting* (New York: Dodd, Mead and Company, 1943), 18.

72 *When he spent Christmas . . . cigars.* David Stafford, *Roosevelt and Churchill: Men of Secrets* (New York: Overlook Press, 1999), 125.

72 *Churchill was so closely . . . reached him.* Roy Howells, *Churchill's Last Years* (New York: David McKay Company, 1965), 192.

73 *"His sensitiveness to effect . . . cigar."* Essay by Sir John Martin, in *Action This Day: Working with Churchill,* ed. John Wheeler-Bennett (New York: St. Martin's Press, 1969), 149.

73 *Once, when asked if . . . day.)* Brian Gardner, *Churchill in Power: As Seen by His Contemporaries* (Boston: Houghton Mifflin Company, 1970), 29.

73 *"I neither want it . . . lifetime."* Kay Halle, *Irrepressible Churchill* (New York: World Publishing Company, 1966), 268.

9: Churchill, True

74 *"Massive, witty, inconsiderate . . . himself."* C. P. Snow, *Variety of Men* (New York: Charles Scribner's Sons, 1966), 169.

75 *"Naught shall make us rue . . . angle.* Margery Allingham, *The Oaken Heart* (London: Michael Joseph Ltd., 1941), 168–70.

10: Churchill's Desire for Fame

77 *"What an awful thing . . . cling to."* Clive Ponting, *Churchill* (London: Sinclair-Stevenson, 1994), 21.

78 *"Every body wants . . . away?"* Randolph S. Churchill, *Winston S. Churchill,* companion vol. 1, part 1 (Boston: Houghton Mifflin Company, 1967), 103.

78 *"I shall be . . . for that,"* Sir Gerald Woods Wollaston, "Churchill at Harrow," in *Churchill by His Contemporaries,* ed. Charles Eade (London: Reprint Society, 1953), 3.

78 *"in the high position . . . Empire."* Martin Gilbert, *In Search of Churchill* (New York: John Wiley & Sons, 1994), 214–15. In 1891.

78 *"having seen service . . . country."* Randolph S. Churchill, *Winston S. Churchill,* companion vol. 1, part 2 (Boston: Houghton Mifflin,

1967), 781. Winston Churchill, letter to his mother, August 29, 1897.

79 *"given an audience . . . different."* Richard Hough, *Winston and Clementine* (New York: Bantam Books, 1990), 79.

79 *"If I am to do . . . offended."* Randolph S. Churchill, *Winston S. Churchill,* companion vol. 1, part 2 (Boston: Houghton Mifflin Company, 1967), 814.

80 *"I am thirty-two . . . though."* Lady Violet Bonham-Carter, *Winston Churchill: An Intimate Portrait* (New York: Harcourt, Brace & World, 1965), 3.

80 *"the war to which . . . life."* Frances Stevenson, *Lloyd George: A Diary* (New York: Harper & Row, 1971), 253. Diary entry of February 13, 1934.

80 *An official at . . . grand.* Lord Alanbrooke, *War Diaries: 1939–1945,* eds. Alex Danchev and Daniel Todman (Berkeley: University of California Press, 2001), 297. Note accompanying entry of August 11, 1942.

80 *"I thought that . . . did not."* A. P. Herbert, *Independent Member* (Garden City: Doubleday and Company, 1951), 94.

81 *"And History, while . . . name."* Winston Churchill, *Savrola* (New York: Random House, 1956), 31.

11: Churchill as Depressive

82 *"When I was young . . . everything."* Lord Moran, *Churchill: Taken from the Diaries of Lord Moran* (Boston: Houghton Mifflin Company, 1966), 179. Diary entry of August 14, 1944.

82 *"I think this man . . . picture."* Martin Gilbert, *In Search of Churchill* (New York: John Wiley & Sons, 1994), 210.

83 *"The worst part . . . suicide."* Earl of Birkenhead, *Churchill, 1874–1922* (London: Harrap, 1990), 392.

83 *During this time . . . moved.* Frances Stevenson, *Lloyd George: A Diary* (New York: Harper & Row, 1971), 253. Diary entry of February 13, 1934.

83 *"at the top of the wheel . . . depression."* Lord Beaverbrook,

Politicians and the War (Garden City: Doubleday, Doran and Company, 1959), 128.

83   *Psychiatrist Anthony Storr . . . relaxation.*   Anthony Storr, *Churchill's Black Dog, Kafka's Mice, and Other Phenomena of the Human Mind* (London: William Collins Sons and Company, 1965), 3–51.

84   *"I was happy . . . a man."*   Winston Churchill, *My Early Life: A Roving Commission* (New York: Charles Scribner's Sons, 1930), 38.

84   *Although Moran's book title . . . diary.*   Gilbert, *In Search of Churchill*, 233.

84   *Gilbert concluded that . . . depression.*   Ibid., 209.

84   *"I thought he would die of grief,"*   Mary Soames, *Clementine Churchill: The Biography of a Marriage* (Boston: Houghton Mifflin Company, 1979), 161.

12: Churchill's Disdain

87   *"You were very rude . . . great man."*   Roy Howells, *Churchill's Last Years* (New York: David McKay Company, 1965), 62.

87   *Action this Day . . . authenticity.*   John Colville, *The Fringes of Power: 10 Downing Street Diaries, 1939–1955* (New York: W. W. Norton & Company, 1985), 280. Diary entry of October 31, 1940.

87   *"no half-way measures . . . into bed."*   Walter Graebner, *My Dear Mr. Churchill* (Boston: Riverside Press, 1965), 45.

88   *"He dressed and . . . like this?' "*   Lucy Masterman, *C.F.G. Masterman: A Biography* (London: Nicholson and Watson, 1939), 97.

88   *"I shall not be far away."*   John Strawson, *Churchill and Hitler: In Victory and Defeat* (New York: Fromm International, 1997), 257.

88   *"I'm quite satisfied . . . continent.*   James Morris, *Farewell the Trumpets: An Imperial Retreat* (New York: Harcourt, Brace and Company, 1978), 298. To Lord Irwin, later Lord Halifax.

89   *"Winston leads general conversation . . . audience."*   Piers Brendon, *Winston Churchill* (New York: Harper & Row, 1984), 37.

89   *"He could become . . . person."*   Dwight D. Eisenhower, "Churchill as an Ally in War," in *Churchill by His Contemporaries*, ed. Charles Eade (London: Reprint Society, 1953), 128.

89 *Not even President Roosevelt . . . tedious."*   Essay by Sir Ian Jacob, in *Action This Day: Working with Churchill,* ed. John Wheeler-Bennett (New York: St. Martin's Press, 1969), 207–8.

89 *"[I]n his many colored . . . gramophone."*   Lord Alanbrooke, *War Diaries: 1939–1945,* eds. Alex Danchev and Daniel Todman (Berkeley: University of California Press, 2001), 194. Diary entry of October 26, 1941.

90 *As a schoolboy at Harrow . . . seen.*   Virginia Cowles, *Winston Churchill: The Era and the Man* (New York: Harper & Brothers, 1953), 36.

90 *"As there was a war on . . . train."*   Kay Halle, *Irrepressible Churchill* (New York: World Publishing Company, 1966), 152.

90 *"I got the best view . . . jacket."*   Martin Gilbert, *Churchill: A Life* (New York: Henry Holt and Company, 1991), 794. Quoting diary entry of secretary Marian Holmes for September 24, 1944.

13: Churchill's Belligerence

93 *"People talked a lot . . . by wars."*   John Colville, *The Fringes of Power: 10 Downing Street Diaries, 1939–1955* (New York: W. W. Norton & Company, 1985), 273. Diary entry of October 22, 1940.

93 *"Look at the Swiss! . . . clock!"*   Kay Halle, *Irrepressible Churchill* (New York: World Publishing Company, 1966), 136. In 1938.

93 *"War is the normal occupation . . . gardening"*   Siegfried Sassoon, *Siegfried's Journey, 1916–1920* (New York: Viking Press, 1946), 119.

93 *"no stone unturned . . . uncooked"*   Winston Churchill, *My Early Life: A Roving Commission* (New York: Charles Scribner's Sons, 1930), 152.

93 *"Nowadays," he complained . . . diplomatist."*   Richard Hough, *Winston and Clementine* (New York: Bantam Books, 1991), 61.

93 *"rode up to individuals . . . doubtful."*   William Manchester, *The Last Lion: Winston Spencer Churchill: Visions of Glory, 1874–1932* (Boston: Little, Brown and Company, 1983), 278.

94 *"It is a shame . . . guns."*   Churchill, *My Early Life,* 64.

94 *"This, this is living . . . give me."*   John Pearson, *The Private Lives of Winston Churchill* (New York: Simon and Schuster, 1991), 146.

94 *In 1922, Clementine . . . face."* Mary Soames, ed., *Winston and Clementine: The Personal Letters of the Churchills* (New York: Houghton Mifflin Company, 1999), 265. Clementine Churchill, letter to Winston Churchill, November 9, 1922.

95 *"Much as war attracts . . . all is."* Ibid., 30. Winston Churchill, letter to Clementine Churchill, September 15, 1909, after he attended German army maneuvers at the Kaiser's invitation.

95 *"This was a time . . . or die."* Winston Churchill, *The Second World War*, vol. 2, *Their Finest Hour* (Boston: Houghton Mifflin Company, 1949), 279.

95 *When he visited . . . days.* Elizabeth Layton Nel, *Mr. Churchill's Secretary* (New York: Coward-McCann, 1958), 53–54.

96 *"We always knew exactly . . . done."* Walter Graebner, *My Dear Mr. Churchill* (Boston: Riverside Press, 1965), 8–9.

96 *"I feel very lonely . . . that?"* Lord Moran, *Churchill: Taken from the Diaries of Lord Moran* (Boston: Houghton Mifflin Company, 1966), 273. Diary entry of June 22, 1945.

96 *During the war, Churchill . . . never used.* Essay by John Colville, in *Action This Day: Working with Churchill,* ed. John Wheeler-Bennett (New York: St. Martin's Press, 1969), 119.

96 *"In great or small station . . . 'Fight on.' "* Martin Gilbert, *Winston S. Churchill*, vol. 3, *The Challenge of War* (Boston: Houghton Mifflin Company, 1971), 694. Winston Churchill, letter to his mother from the trenches, January 29, 1916.

96 *"Nations as well as . . . founded."* Winston Churchill, *The World Crisis,* vol. 3 (New York: Charles Scribner's Sons, 1927), 217.

15: Churchill as Son

103 *"The greatest and most powerful . . . memory."* Winston Churchill, *Amid These Storms* (New York: Charles Scribner's Sons, 1932), 51–52.

104 *"Waiter—please listen . . . story."* Lady Violet Bonham-Carter, *Winston Churchill: An Intimate Portrait* (New York: Harcourt, Brace & World, 1965), 269, asterisked note.

104 *Only nine years later . . . death.* John Mather, "Lord Randolph

Churchill: Maladies et Mort," *Finest Hour: The Journal of the Churchill Center and International Churchill Societies* 93 (winter 1996–1997): 23–28.

105 *"This is a letter which . . . style."* Keith Alldritt, *Churchill the Writer: His Life as a Man of Letters* (London: Hutchinson, 1992), 2.

105 *"What fun it would be . . . Foot."* Winston Churchill, *My Early Life: A Roving Commission* (New York: Charles Scribner's Sons, 1930), 35.

105 *[In failing to qualify . . . existence.* Randolph Churchill, *Winston S. Churchill,* companion vol. 1, part 1 (Boston: Houghton Mifflin Company, 1967), 390–391. Randolph Churchill, letter to Winston Churchill, August 9, 1893.

105 *"He seemed to own . . . stone."* Churchill, *My Early Life,* 46.

106 *"All my dreams . . . memory."* Ibid., 62.

106 *"incessant complaints . . . application."* Randolph Churchill, *Churchill,* companion vol. 1, part 1, 390.

106 *He spent twenty minutes . . . the Bar.* Churchill, *My Early Life,* 19.

107 *"I cannot sit down . . . preserve."* James C. Humes, *Churchill: Speaker of the Century* (New York: Stein and Day, 1980), 80.

107 *"This fulfils my ambition . . . Chancellor."* Martin Gilbert, *Churchill: A Life* (New York: Henry Holt and Company, 1991), 465.

107 *In 1947, during a family . . . course."* Martin Gilbert, *In Search of Churchill* (New York: John Wiley & Sons, 1994), 315.

108 *At the end of his life . . . father.* Lord Moran, *Churchill: Taken from the Diaries of Lord Moran* (Boston: Houghton Mifflin Company, 1966), 814.

16: Churchill as Father

109 *He often read . . . stories.* Martin Gilbert, *In Search of Churchill* (New York: John Wiley & Sons, 1994), 205.

110 *"I pass through again . . . life."* Mary Soames, *Clementine Churchill: The Biography of a Marriage* (Boston: Houghton Mifflin Company, 1979), 269. Winston Churchill, letter to Clementine Churchill, August 14, 1922.

110 *"You are the best . . . stand."* Gilbert, *In Search*, 207–8.

111 *"We soon became aware . . . trivial."* Soames, *Clementine Churchill*, 313.

111 *"great guns but no ammunition."* Norman Rose, *Churchill: The Unruly Giant* (New York: Free Press, 1994), 257.

111 *Randolph bellowed at his . . . whiskey.* Winston S. Churchill, *His Father's Son: The Life of Randolph Churchill* (London: Weidenfeld & Nicolson, 1996), 389.

17: Churchill the Painter

113 *"To be really happy . . . hobbies."* Winston Churchill, *Painting as a Pastime* (New York: Cornerstone, 1950), 8.

113 *Many remedies are suggested . . . coat.* Ibid., 7.

114 *Churchill painted only one picture . . . Roosevelt.* David Coombs, *Churchill: His Paintings* (catalog) (New York: World Publishing Company, 1967), plate 54 (381), *Tower of Katoubia Mosque,* 1943.

115 *"In this position . . . pressure."* Churchill, *Painting as a Pastime,* 16.

116 *"Every ambition I've ever had . . . painter."* Walter Graebner, *My Dear Mr. Churchill* (Boston: Riverside Press, 1965), 83.

116 *Churchill loved his own . . . museums.* William Manchester, *The Last Lion: Winston Spencer Churchill: Visions of Glory, 1874–1932* (Boston: Little, Brown and Company, 1983), 761.

117 *"the horrors of war . . . the sun."* Martin Gilbert, *In Search of Churchill* (New York: John Wiley & Sons, 1994), 76.

117 *("I rejoice with . . . browns")* Churchill, *Painting as a Pastime,* 24.

117 *("Now I am learning . . . sunshine")* Ibid., 32.

117 *"The colours are lovely . . . absorbing."* Ibid., 19.

117 *"[h]e would have eaten . . . of it so."* Gilbert, *In Search,* 76.

118 *"Happy are the painters . . . the day."* Churchill, *Painting as a Pastime,* 13.

18: Churchill the Spendthrift

120 *"If I had not been . . . now."* Randolph S. Churchill, *Winston S. Churchill,* companion vol. 1, part 1 (Boston: Houghton Mifflin Company, 1967), 672.

120 *"throughout his life . . . answered"* Lady Violet Bonham-Carter, *Winston Churchill: An Intimate Portrait* (New York: Harcourt, Brace & World, 1965), 107.

120 *In the early days . . . skin.* Ibid., 173.

121 *[D]o not worry . . . trifles.* Mary Soames: *Clementine Churchill: The Biography of a Marriage* (Boston: Houghton Mifflin Company, 1979), 304.

121 *"I have always had . . . friend."* Bonham-Carter, *An Intimate Portrait*, 107.

122 *From youth until . . . debt.* David Cannadine, *Aspects of Aristocracy* (New York: Penguin Books, 1994), 144.

19: Conflicting Views of Churchill

127 *One of the . . . forthcoming.* Clementine Churchill, letter to Winston Churchill, June 27, 1940, Churchill Archives Centre, Baroness Spencer-Churchill Papers, CSCT 1-24.

20: Churchill in Tears

132 *"Then Lloyd George gets up . . . eyes."* Harold Nicolson, *Diaries and Letters,* vol. 2, *The War Years, 1939–1945,* ed. Nigel Nicolson (New York: Atheneum, 1967), 85. Diary entry of May 13, 1940.

132 *"The grand finale . . . cheeks."* Ibid., 100. Diary entry of July 4, 1940.

132 *"We had two lovely films . . . comedy."* Diana Cooper, *Trumpets from the Steep* (Boston: Houghton Mifflin Company, 1960), 69.

132 *"Churchill was affected . . . pocket."* Brian Gardner, *Churchill in Power: As Seen by His Contemporaries* (Boston: Houghton Mifflin Company, 1970), 130, quoting journalist H. V. Morton, writing about the Atlantic Meeting.

132 *"[H]e quotes Kipling's lines . . . continue."* Nicolson, *Diaries and Letters*, September 9, 1941.

132 *"We then find him . . . face!"* Lord Alanbrooke, *War Diaries: 1939–1945*, eds. Alex Danchev and Daniel Todman (Berkeley: University of California Press, 2001), 324. Note accompanying entry of September 24, 1942.

132 *"Not for one moment . . . Paris."* Nicolson, *Diaries and Letters*, November 14, 1944.

133 *"Before [a speaker] can . . . flow."* Randolph S. Churchill, *Winston S. Churchill*, companion vol. 1, part 2 (Boston: Houghton Mifflin Company, 1967), 818. Quoting Churchill's unpublished 1897 essay "The Scaffolding of Rhetoric."

133 *Already little pathetic Union Jacks . . . admiration.* Winston Churchill, *The Second World War,* vol. 2, *Their Finest Hour* (Boston: Houghton Mifflin Company, 1949), 348.

134 *"There had been heavy fighting . . . so moved."* Lord Ismay, *The Memoirs of General Lord Ismay* (New York: Viking Press, 1960), 179–80.

134 *"would break my heart."* David Kennedy, *Freedom from Fear: The American People in Depression and War, 1929–1945* (New York: Oxford University Press, 1999), 574.

134 *"I do not think . . . House."* Andrew Barrow, *Gossip: A History of High Society from 1920 to 1970* (New York: Coward, McCann & Geoghegan, 1978), 130.

134 *"Sweet cat—I kiss . . . love—W."* Mary Soames, ed., *Winston and Clementine: The Personal Letters of the Churchills* (New York: Houghton Mifflin Company, 1999), 30. Winston Churchill, letter to Clementine Churchill, September 15, 1909.

135 *"I have nothing to offer . . . sweat,"* Roy Jenkins, *Churchill* (New York: Farrar, Straus and Giroux, 2001), 591.

21: Churchill the Drinker

136 *In the space of . . . as well.* Clive Ponting, *Churchill* (London: Sinclair-Stevenson, 1994), 726.

137 *"A tumbler was brought . . . 7:30 A.M."* Lord Alanbrooke, *War Diaries: 1939–1945*, eds. Alex Danchev and Daniel Todman (Berkeley: University of California Press, 2001), 370. Note accompanying entry of January 26, 1943.

137 *"We had to consider . . . dictated it."* Ibid., 683. Diary entry of April 12, 1945.

137 *With the Grenadier Guards . . . headquarters.* Winston Churchill,

Amid These Storms (New York: Charles Scribner's Sons, 1932), 104–5.

137 *"This is to certify . . . times."* William Manchester, *The Last Lion: Winston Spencer Churchill: Visions of Glory, 1874–1932* (Boston: Little, Brown and Company, 1983), 880–81.

138 *"The glass of weak whisky . . . hours."* Martin Gilbert, *In Search of Churchill* (New York: John Wiley & Sons, 1994), 209, quoting John Peck.

138 *"He was never the worse . . . morning."* Essay by Sir Ian Jacob, in *Action This Day: Working with Churchill*, ed. John Wheeler-Bennett (New York: St. Martin's Press, 1969), 183.

138 *"My rule of life . . . them."* Brian Gardner, *Churchill in Power: As Seen by His Contemporaries* (Boston: Houghton Mifflin Company, 1970), 277.

138 *"When I was younger . . . breakfast."* Kay Halle, *Irrepressible Churchill* (New York: World Publishing Company, 1966), 268.

22: Churchill in Context

143 *"because he was . . . conquerors."* Virginia Cowles, *Winston Churchill: The Era and the Man* (New York: Harper & Brothers, 1953), 8.

145 *For while the tired waves . . . bright.* Arthur Hugh Clough, *The Poems of Arthur Hugh Clough* (New York: Oxford University Press, 1968), 63.

23: Churchill and Sex

148 *"strong sexual desires."* John Colville, *Winston Churchill and His Inner Circle* (New York: Wyndham Books, 1981), 143.

148 *"the reason I can write . . . in bed."* Norman Rose, *Churchill: The Unruly Giant* (New York: Free Press, 1994), 254.

148 *Historians William Manchester . . . development.* William Manchester, *The Last Lion: William Spencer Churchill: Alone, 1932–1940* (Boston: Little, Brown and Company, 1988), 15.

149 *"acts of gross immorality . . . type."* William Manchester, *The Last*

Lion: William Spencer Churchill: Visions of Glory, 1874–1932 (Boston: Little, Brown and Company, 1983), 212.

149 *"with a divorced . . . his."* Manchester, *Alone*, 15.

149 *"absolutely obsessed with a senile passion . . . walk."* Noël Coward, *The Noël Coward Diaries,* eds. Graham Payn and Sheridan Morley (Boston: Little, Brown and Company, 1982), 323. Diary entry of June 9, 1956.

24: Churchill as Husband

153 *Oh my darling . . . romances.* Martin Gilbert, *Winston S. Churchill,* vol. 3, *The Challenge of War* (Boston: Houghton Mifflin Company, 1971), 744–45.

153 *"at least until September 1908 . . . afterwards."* Winston Churchill, *My Early Life* (New York: Charles Scribner's Sons, 1930), 372.

153 *"Breakfast should be had . . . alone,"* Walter Graebner, *My Dear Mr. Churchill* (Boston: Riverside Press, 1965), 46.

155 *"it was almost incredible . . . life."* Roy Jenkins, *Churchill* (New York: Farrar, Straus and Giroux, 2001), 786, asterisked note.

25: Churchill's Island Story

157 *"that she thought [Winston] . . . was not."* Essay by John Colville, in *Action This Day: Working with Churchill,* ed. John Wheeler-Bennett (New York: St. Martin's Press, 1969), 75–76.

158 *He adopted a . . . parts."* Winston Churchill, *The Second World War,* vol. 6, *Triumph and Tragedy* (Boston: Houghton Mifflin Company, 1953), 752–53.

159 *"on waking up . . . the day."* Essay by Lord Normanbrook, in *Action This Day,* 41.

159 *This royal throne . . . England.* William Shakespeare, *The Tragedy of King Richard II,* 2.1.40–45.

26: Churchill in Photographs

165 *September 1940. Winston and Clementine . . . favorites.* Mary Soames, *Family Album* (Boston: Houghton Mifflin Company, 1982), photograph 262.

169 *"In all our long . . . than this."* Winston Churchill, *War Speeches,* vol. 5, *Victory* (Boston: Little, Brown and Company, 1946), 167.

27: Churchill as the Hero of a Novel

171 *"A human life is . . . force."* André Maurois, *Aspects of Biography* (New York: D. Appleton and Company, 1929), 71.

173 *At age seventy . . . fringe.* William Manchester, *The Last Lion: William Spencer Churchill: Alone, 1932–1940* (Boston: Little, Brown and Company, 1988), 24.

173 *"My career is a failure . . . offer"* A.J.P. Taylor, *The Warlords* (New York: Atheneum, 1978), 72.

173 *"Winston won't last . . . beginning."* Andrew Roberts, *Eminent Churchillians* (New York: Simon and Schuster, 1994), 159, quoting Robert Bruce Lockhart's diary, May 21, 1940, recording that MP Peter Eckersley said, "Winston won't last five months! Opposition from Tories is already beginning."

174 *"He is a man who leads . . . leadership"* Raymond Callahan, *Churchill: Retreat from Empire* (Wilmington: Scholarly Resources, 1984), 11, quoting Harold Nicolson, 1931, *Vanity Fair.*

174 *"No, unless some . . . for that"* Mary Soames, *Clementine Churchill: The Biography of a Marriage* (Boston: Houghton Mifflin Company, 1979), 361.

174 *"I represent to them . . . cheer me,"* John Colville, *The Fringes of Power: 10 Downing Street Diaries, 1939–1955* (New York: W. W. Norton & Company, 1985), 275. Diary entry of October 24, 1940.

174 *"There is one thing . . . ready."* Richard Hough, *Winston and Clementine* (New York: Bantam Books, 1988), 285.

174 *"His Majesty the King . . . six P.M."* Ibid., 407.

176 *Churchill loved champagne . . . scalps.* Lord Alanbrooke, *War Diaries: 1939–1945,* eds. Alex Danchev and Daniel Todman (Berkeley: University of California Press, 2001), 667–68, note accompanying March 3, 1945; Kay Halle, *Irrepressible Churchill* (New York: World Publishing Company, 1966), 108.

176 *"most overworked word" . . . "prod."* Phyllis Moir, *I Was Winston Churchill's Private Secretary* (New York: Wilfred Funk, Inc., 1941), 121.

28: Churchill's Destiny

179   *Asked why he expected . . . forty-six.*   Lady Violet Bonham-Carter, *Winston Churchill: An Intimate Portrait* (New York: Harcourt, Brace & World, 1965), 10.

179   *"I am so conceited . . . ending."*   Randolph S. Churchill, *Winston S. Churchill*, companion vol. 1, part 2 (Boston: Houghton Mifflin Company, 1967), 839.

179   *"Above all don't be . . . surely."*   Mary Soames, ed., *Winston and Clementine: The Personal Letters of the Churchills* (New York: Houghton Mifflin Company, 1999), 120. Winston Churchill, letter to Clementine Churchill, November 27, 1915.

180   *"Death in Revelation . . . me!"*   Winston Churchill, *My Early Life: A Roving Commission* (New York: Charles Scribner's Sons, 1930), 340.

181   *"Cheek!"*   Andrew Barrow, *Gossip: A History of High Society from 1920 to 1970* (New York: Coward, McCann & Geoghegan, 1978), 129.

181   *"I was conscious of . . . trial."*   Winston Churchill, *The Second World War,* vol. 1, *The Gathering Storm* (Boston: Houghton Mifflin Company 1948), 667.

181   *"It certainly was odd . . . plan."*   Winston Churchill, *The Second World War*, vol. 3, *The Grand Alliance* (Boston: Houghton Mifflin Company, 1950), 671.

181   *You never can tell . . . decision.*   Churchill, *My Early Life*, 102.

182   *"I could not be reproached . . . invisible wings."*   Churchill, *Gathering Storm*, 667, 181.

182   *By the end of the meeting . . . inevitable.*   For lengthier discussion of the choice of Churchill over Halifax to succeed Chamberlain, see Andrew Roberts, *"The Holy Fox": The Life of Lord Halifax* (London: Phoenix Giant, 1991), 197–209; Roy Jenkins, *Churchill* (New York: Farrar, Straus and Giroux, 2001), 583–87.

183   *Perhaps he believed . . . Foreign Secretary,*   Roberts, *Holy Fox*, 199.

183   *or perhaps he predicted . . . removed.*   Jenkins, *Churchill*, 585.

184   *This was a man who . . . appointment.*   Roberts, *Holy Fox*, 208.

184   *"might well have succeeded . . . fanatic."*   Keith Feiling, *The Life of Neville Chamberlain* (Hamden: Archon Books, 1970), 452.

185 *"Chance, Fortune, Luck . . . power."*   Winston Churchill, *Amid These Storms* (New York: Charles Scribner's Sons, 1932), 106.

29: Churchill the Imperialist

187 *"I was brought up . . . unequal."*   Lord Moran, *Churchill: Taken from the Diaries of Lord Moran* (Boston: Houghton Mifflin Company, 1966), 576.

187 *I am sure . . . today.*   Raymond Callahan, *Churchill: Retreat from Empire* (Wilmington: Scholarly Resources, 1984), 28.

188 *He wrote the Secretary . . . subject."*   Winston Churchill, *The Second World War*, vol. 6, *Triumph and Tragedy* (Boston: Houghton Mifflin Company, 1953), 692.

188 *"Why be apologetic . . . superior."*   Christopher Thorne, *Allies of a Kind* (New York: Oxford University Press, 1978), xxiii.

188 *"When you learn to think . . . white man."*   Moran, *Diaries*, 394. Diary entry of January 19, 1952.

188 *"far above anything . . . maintain"*   Andrew Roberts, *Eminent Churchillians* (New York: Simon and Schuster, 1994), 214.

188 *"It is alarming . . . exposed."*   David Cannadine, ed., *Blood, Toil, Tears, and Sweat: The Speeches of Winston Churchill* (Boston: Houghton Mifflin Company, 1989), 103.

189 *"No lover,"* Churchill said *. . . Roosevelt."*   Roy Jenkins, *Churchill* (New York: Farrar, Straus and Giroux, 2001), 784.

189 *"Mr. President, with . . . now."*   Winston Churchill, *The Second World War*, vol. 2, *Their Finest Hour* (New York: Houghton Mifflin Company, 1949), 402.

190 *The United States stands . . . in war.*   Cannadine, *Blood, Toil, Tears, and Sweat*, 296–97.

190 *The answer might also . . . independence.*   Callahan, *Retreat from Empire*, 255.

191 *The United States stand . . . history.*   Winston Churchill, *War Speeches*, vol. 5, *Victory* (Boston: Little, Brown and Company, 1946), 295.

191 *"The [United States's] Constitution . . . American."*   Winston

Churchill, *A History of the English-Speaking Peoples,* vol. 3, *The Age of Revolution* (New York: Dodd, Mead and Company, 1957), 256.

191 *"I have not become . . . Empire."* Winston Churchill, *War Speeches,* vol. 2, *The End of the Beginning* (Boston: Little, Brown and Company, 1943), 268. Winston Churchill's Guildhall speech of November 10, 1942.

192 *"It is with deep grief . . . herself."* Clive Ponting, *Churchill* (London: Sinclair-Stevenson, 1994), 741.

192 *"Of course he was depressed . . . Empire."* Anita Leslie, *Clare Sheridan* (Garden City: Doubleday and Company, 1977), 299.

192 *"In the end . . . gone."* Ibid., 304–5.

31: Churchill and Roosevelt

198 *"It is fun . . . as you."* John Lukacs, *Churchill: Visionary. Statesman. Historian.* (New Haven: Yale University Press, 2002), 56.

199 *"the most unsordid . . . nation."* David Kennedy, *Freedom from Fear: The American People in Depression and War, 1929–1945* (New York: Oxford University Press, 1999), 475.

201 *"we are not only . . . bone."* Clive Ponting, *Churchill* (London: Sinclair-Stevenson, 1994), 510.

32: Churchill's Imagination

202 *"The fortunate generations . . . unlucky."* Lytton Strachey, *Biographical Essays* (New York: Harcourt, Brace and Company, 1949), "Charles Greville," 243.

203 *"the hero of five wars . . . Britain."* John Pearson, *The Private Lives of Winston Churchill* (New York: Simon and Schuster, 1991), 105.

203 *One evening in August . . . in 1066.* A.J.P. Taylor, *The Warlords* (New York: Atheneum, 1978), 86–87.

205 *Few had shared his belief . . . Moscow.* John Colville, *Winston Churchill and His Inner Circle* (New York: Wyndham Books, 1981), 213.

205 *Prime Minister to First Lord . . . morning.* Winston Churchill, *The Second World War,* vol. 2, *Their Finest Hour* (Boston: Houghton Mifflin Company, 1949), 465.

205 *in 1944, when Churchill . . . Gibraltar.* Winston Churchill, *The*

Second World War, vol. 6, *Triumph and Tragedy* (Boston: Houghton Mifflin Company, 1953), 703. Memorandum to Colonial Secretary, September 1, 1944.

206 *"These are my story . . . let him."* Lord Tedder, *With Prejudice: The War Memoirs* (Boston: Little, Brown and Company, 1966), i.

207 *He admitted that . . . mistakes,* Brian Gardner, *Churchill in Power: As Seen by His Contemporaries* (Boston: Houghton Mifflin Company, 1970), 218, quoting Captain H. C. Butcher, naval aide to Eisenhower, diary of May 31, 1943.

207 *Future generations may deem . . . issues.* Winston Churchill, *The Second World War,* vol. 2, *Their Finest Hour* (Boston: Houghton Mifflin Company, 1949), 177.

208 *"We sallied forth . . . hold it."* Winston Churchill, *The Second World War,* vol. 4, *The Hinge of Fate* (Boston: Houghton Mifflin Company, 1950), 516.

208 *One of his much-studied . . . Awaits."* Colville, *Inner Circle,* 187.

208 *Churchill wrote with . . . of it."* Churchill, *The Hinge of Fate,* 596.

209 *"I leave the judgment . . . history."* Gardner, *Churchill in Power,* 72.

209 *Meeting with Stalin . . . keep it."* Winston Churchill, *The Second World War,* vol. 6, *Triumph and Tragedy* (Boston: Houghton Mifflin Company, 1953), 227–28.

209 *he insisted that . . . race."* Churchill, *The Hinge of Fate,* 100. In fact, Churchill did permit the British commander to surrender to the Japanese.

210 *"Everything I was sure . . . happened."* Winston Churchill, *My Early Life: A Roving Commission* (New York: Charles Scribner's Sons, 1930), 67.

33: Churchill and Hitler

212 *"a horror of whistling"* John Colville, *The Fringes of Power: 10 Downing Street Diaries, 1939–1955* (New York: W. W. Norton & Company 1985), 158. Diary entry of June 15, 1940.

213 *I am willing to sign . . . demands it?* John Strawson, *Churchill and Hitler: In Victory and Defeat* (New York: Fromm International, 1997), 203.

214   *"few, if any . . . 1933."*   Ian Kershaw, *The "Hitler Myth": Image and Reality in the Third Reich* (New York: Oxford University Press, 1987), 1.

214   *"Are we beasts? . . . too far?"*   Piers Brendon, *Winston Churchill: A Biography* (New York: Harper & Row, 1984), 190.

214   *"I hate nobody . . . professional."*   John Colville, *Winston Churchill and His Inner Circle* (New York: Wyndham Books, 1981), 11.

214   *I am free to confess . . . appals me.*   Mary Soames, ed., *Winston and Clementine: The Personal Letters of the Churchills* (New York: Houghton Mifflin Company, 1999), 512. Winston Churchill, letter to Clementine Churchill, February 1, 1945.

215   *"Close your hearts . . . right."*   Ian Kershaw, *Hitler, 1936–1945: Nemesis* (New York: W. W. Norton & Company, 2000), 209.

215   *"Losses can never . . . greatness."*   John Strawson, *Churchill and Hitler: In Victory and Defeat* (New York: Fromm International, 1997), 207.

216   *wrote General Ismay to . . . brigades."*   Winston Churchill, *The Second World War*, vol. 6, *Triumph and Tragedy* (Boston: Houghton Mifflin Company, 1953), 732.

216   *The whole fury . . . finest hour."*   David Cannadine, ed., *Blood, Toil, Tears, and Sweat: The Speeches of Winston Churchill* (Boston: Houghton Mifflin Company, 1989), 177–78.

216   *"I never gave them . . . theirs."*   Diana Cooper, *Trumpets from the Steep* (Boston: Houghton Mifflin Company, 1960), 69.

217   *"We can no longer afford . . . population."*   Albert Speer, *Inside the Third Reich,* trans. Richard and Clara Winston (New York: Touchstone, 1970), 439.

217   *"A talk by the Fuhrer . . . the same."*   Joseph Goebbels, *Final Entries 1945: The Diaries of Joseph Goebbels,* ed. Hugh Trevor-Roper, trans. Richard Barry (New York: G. P. Putnam's Sons, 1978), 237. Diary entry of March 26, 1945.

217   *"Hitler's gifts as an orator . . . illusions."*   Alan Bullock, *Hitler: A Study in Tyranny* (New York: HarperPerennial, 1962), 423–24.

217   *"If the war is . . . nation."*   H. R. Trevor-Roper, *The Last Days of Hitler* (New York: Macmillan Company, 1947), 82.

218 *"But had this war . . . Churchill?"* Brian Gardner, *Churchill in Power: As Seen by His Contemporaries* (Boston: Houghton Mifflin Company, 1910), 150. Hitler broadcast of January 30, 1942.

219 *It almost causes . . . destroy.* John Strawson, *Churchill and Hitler: In Victory and Defeat* (New York: Fromm International, 1997), 277.

34: Churchill Exposed

222 *"glad to record" . . . people."* Winston Churchill, *The Second World War*, vol. 6, *Triumph and Tragedy* (Boston: Houghton Mifflin Company, 1953), 150.

222 *whether "blacks . . . production.' "* Lord Moran, *Churchill: Taken from the Diaries of Lord Moran* (Boston: Houghton Mifflin Company, 1966), 692. Diary entry of April 8, 1955.

222 *"Winston regarded males . . . male sex?"* Anita Leslie, *Clare Sheridan* (Garden City: Doubleday and Company, 1977), 42.

222 *"contrary to natural law . . . states"* Randolph S. Churchill, *Winston S. Churchill*, companion vol. 1, part 2 (Boston: Houghton Mifflin Company, 1967), 765.

222 *"adequately represented by their husbands."* Ibid.

222 *Later, he supported . . . consistent.* William Manchester, *The Last Lion: Winston Spencer Churchill: Visions of Glory, 1874–1932* (Boston: Little, Brown and Company, 1983), 245, 375.

223 *as late as the 1930s . . . elements."* David Cannadine, *Aspects of Aristocracy* (New York: Penguin Books, 1994), 158.

223 *"we had a real . . . set in."* Winston Churchill, *My Early Life: A Roving Commission* (New York: Charles Scribner's Sons, 1930), 359.

223 *"The unnatural and increasingly . . . exaggerate."* Clive Ponting, *Churchill* (London: Sinclair-Stevenson, 1994), 101–2; private letter to Prime Minister Asquith.

223 *Years later, a young . . . at a time."* William Manchester, *The Last Lion: William Spencer Churchill: Alone, 1932–1940* (Boston: Little, Brown and Company, 1988), 109.

225 *He ordered studies . . . towns.* Roy Jenkins, *Churchill* (New York: Farrar, Straus and Giroux, 2001), 747.

35: Churchill True or False

227 *When Churchill was captured . . . prisoner.* False. Richard Hough, *Winston and Clementine* (New York: Bantam Books, 1991), 109, explains that Field Cornet Oosthuizen, not Botha, made the capture.

227 *Churchill didn't see* Hamlet *. . . seventies.* Clive Ponting, *Churchill* (London: Sinclair-Stevenson, 1994), 43.

227 *Churchill altered his . . . Eisenhower.* John Colville, *The Fringes of Power: 10 Downing Street Diaries, 1939–1955* (New York: W. W. Norton & Company, 1985), 658. Diary entry of January 1, 1953.

228 *Churchill was a Freemason.* From 1901 to 1912. Ponting, *Churchill,* 43.

228 *Out of superstition . . . table.* Walter Graebner, *My Dear Mr. Churchill* (Boston: Riverside Press, 1965), 51.

228 *Churchill's great-granddaughter . . . attendants.* Churchill, whose full name was Winston Leonard Spencer-Churchill, and Princess Diana, the former Lady Diana Frances Spencer, were distant cousins related through the Spencer line, descendants of the first Duchess of Marlborough. Churchill's five-year-old great-granddaughter had been Diana's kindergarten pupil.

228 *Clementine once threw . . . head.* Mary Soames, *Clementine Churchill: The Biography of a Marriage* (Boston: Houghton Mifflin Company, 1979), 305.

228 *Clementine once sold . . . expenses.* David Cannadine, *Aspects of Aristocracy* (New York: Penguin Books, 1994), 145.

229 *When Churchill returned . . . back."* False. Martin Gilbert, *In Search of Churchill* (New York: John Wiley & Sons, 1994), 232. Biographer Martin Gilbert, who wrote the exhaustive and authoritative life of Churchill, could find no record to show that this famous message had ever actually been sent.

229 *When reports indicated . . . sending aid.* False. Ibid., 684.

230 *Churchill sent £2 . . . servant.* James Morris, *Farewell the Trumpets: An Imperial Retreat* (New York: Harcourt, Brace and Company, 1978), 546.

230 *As First Lord in 1940 . . . capture.* William Manchester, *The Last*

Lion: William Spencer Churchill: Alone, 1932–1940 (Boston: Little, Brown and Company, 1988), 553.

231   *Churchill once traveled . . . luggage.*   Andrew Barrow, *Gossip: A History of High Society from 1920 to 1970* (New York: Coward, McCann & Geoghegan, 1978), 175.

231   *"I have a keen . . . dervishes."*   Randolph S. Churchill, *Winston S. Churchill*, companion vol. 1, part 2 (Boston: Houghton Mifflin Company, 1967), 963. Winston Churchill, letter to his mother, August 10, 1898.

231   *"I do not care so much . . . give me."*   Ibid., 933. Winston Churchill, letter to his mother, May 16, 1898.

231   *"No one can travel . . . degradation."*   Winston Churchill, *My African Journey* (New York: George H. Doran Company, 1908), 37–38.

231   *"I only wish . . . soul."*   Mary Soames, ed., *Winston and Clementine: The Personal Letters of the Churchills* (New York: Houghton Mifflin Company, 1999), 81. Winston Churchill, letter to Clementine Churchill, November 3, 1913.

231   *"We have got . . . to us."*   Winston Churchill to Cabinet, January 10, 1914.

232   *Of the Navy . . . lash!"*   False. See Gilbert, *In Search*, 232.

232   *"I know this war . . . I live."*   Lady Violet Bonham-Carter, *Winston Churchill: An Intimate Portrait* (New York: Harcourt, Brace & World, 1965), 295; in 1915.

232   *"As to freedom . . . government?"*   Piers Brendon, *Winston Churchill: A Biography* (New York: Harper & Row, 1984), 105.

232   *"A universal suffrage . . . great."*   Essay by Robert Rhodes James, in *Churchill: A Major New Assessment of His Life in Peace and War,* eds. Robert Blake and William Roger Louis (Boston: Houghton Mifflin Company, 1993), 114.

232   *"India is no more . . . Equator."*   Winston Churchill, speech at the Constitution Club, March 11, 1931.

232   *"Thus the world lives . . . age."*   Winston Churchill, *Great Contemporaries* (Chicago: University of Chicago Press, 1937), "Hitler and His Choice," 268.

232 *"The greatest cross . . . Lorraine."* False. Gilbert, *In Search,* 233.

233 *"Kindly remember I am . . . train."* Ponting, *Churchill,* 730. Churchill remark upon learning that a train was not scheduled to stop in Annecy, from which he wished to leave.

233 *"We have now reached . . . fifteen."* Winston Churchill, *A History of the English-Speaking Peoples,* vol. 2, *The New World* (New York: Dodd, Mead and Company, 1956), 3. This curious observation is the first line of the volume.

36: The Tragedy of Winston Churchill, Englishman

237 *"A man larger than . . . our time."* Isaiah Berlin, *Mr. Churchill in 1940* (Boston: Houghton Mifflin Company, 1949), 39.

237 *"His spirit is indomitable . . . privateers."* John Colville, *The Fringes of Power: 10 Downing Street Diaries, 1939–1955* (New York: W. W. Norton & Company, 1985), 136. Diary entry of May 19, 1940.

237 *"The life he lived . . . the end."* Winston Churchill, *Savrola* (New York: Random House, 1956), 32.

238 *Instead, under Churchill . . . war's end.* Robert Skidelsky, *John Maynard Keynes,* vol. 3, *Fighting for Freedom, 1937–1946* (New York: Viking, 2000), 125, 142.

239 *"I have always faithfully . . . life."* Winston Churchill, *Maxims and Reflections,* ed. Colin Coote (Boston: Houghton Mifflin Company, 1947), 33.

239 *"We answered all the tests . . . useless."* Lord Moran, *Churchill: Taken from the Diaries of Lord Moran* (Boston: Houghton Mifflin Company, 1966), 744. Diary entry of June 19, 1956.

239 *"I have achieved much . . . the end."* Sarah Churchill, *A Thread in the Tapestry* (London: André Deutsch, 1967), 17.

239 *"In the end . . . gone."* Anita Leslie, *Clare Sheridan* (Garden City: Doubleday and Company, 1977), 304–5.

240 *"life is at bottom . . . powerful,"* Friedrich Nietzsche, *The Birth of Tragedy and the Genealogy of Morals* (Garden City: Doubleday and Company, 1956), 50.

37: Churchill in Portrait

243   *"gross & cruel monster."*   Mary Soames, *Clementine Churchill: The Biography of a Marriage* (Boston: Houghton Mifflin Company, 1979), 666.

243   *"The portrait is . . . candour."*   Ibid., 588.

244   *Clementine secretly destroyed it . . . again.*   Ibid., 664.

244   *"I feel like an aeroplane . . . landing."*   Norman Rose, *Churchill: The Unruly Giant* (New York: Free Press, 1994), 414.

38: Churchill's Last Days

246   *"He died in harness . . . his!"*   Winston Churchill, *War Speeches*, vol. 5, *Victory* (Boston: Little, Brown and Company, 1946), 137. Eulogy in the House of Commons, April 17, 1945.

247   *"I never think of . . . have."*   Diana Cooper, *Trumpets from the Steep* (Boston: Houghton Mifflin Company, 1960), 189.

247   *He spent hours listening . . . player.*   Roy Howells, *Churchill's Last Years* (New York: David McKay Company, 1965), 169.

247   *"Blessings become curses," he said . . . and now . . ."*   Lord Moran, *Churchill: Taken from the Diaries of Lord Moran* (Boston: Houghton Mifflin Company, 1966), 311.

247   *"I've got to kill . . . ended."*   Martin Gilbert, *Churchill: A Life* (New York: Henry Holt and Company, 1991), 956.

247   *"Today is the twenty-fourth . . . too."*   John Colville, *Winston Churchill and His Inner Circle* (New York: Wyndham Books, 1981), 30.

248   *"I'm so bored with it all."*   Mary Soames, *Clementine Churchill: The Biography of a Marriage* (Boston: Houghton Mifflin Company, 1979), 646.

249   *"Nineteen-forty . . . every time."*   Moran, *Diaries*, 348. Diary entry of December 7, 1947.

249   *He had planned to be . . . father.*   Ibid., 814. Diary entry of December 16, 1959.

SELECT BIBLIOGRAPHY

Forty Ways to Look at Winston Churchill rests on the work of more comprehensive biographers. It was a pleasure to draw upon the huge, fascinating literature about Winston Churchill and his time, and I hope my brief account of Churchill's life will inspire readers to read further. Listed here are principal works consulted as well as sources related to the study of biography.

The most authoritative account of Churchill's life is the eight-volume biography with companion volumes of relevant documents, begun by Randolph Churchill and completed by Martin Gilbert (1966–1988).

Alanbrooke, Lord. *War Diaries: 1939–1945*. Edited by Alex Danchev and Daniel Todman. Berkeley: University of California Press, 2001.

Alldritt, Keith. *Churchill the Writer: His Life as a Man of Letters*. London: Hutchinson, 1992.

Allingham, Margery. *The Oaken Heart*. London: Michael Joseph Ltd., 1941.

Ashley, Maurice. *Churchill as Historian*. New York: Charles Scribner's Sons, 1968.

Backscheider, Paula R. *Reflections on Biography*. Oxford: Oxford University Press, 2001.

Barnes, Julian. *Flaubert's Parrot*. New York: Vintage International, 1984.

Barrow, Andrew. *Gossip: A History of High Society from 1920 to 1970*. New York: Coward, McCann & Geoghegan, 1978.

Beaton, Cecil. *The Years Between: Diaries, 1939–1944*. New York: Holt, Rinehart and Winston, 1965.

Berlin, Sir Isaiah. *The Hedgehog and the Fox*. Chicago: Elephant Paperback, 1953.

———. *Mr. Churchill in 1940*. Boston: Houghton Mifflin Company, 1949.

Best, Geoffrey. *Churchill: A Study in Greatness*. London: Hambledon and London, 2001.

Birkenhead, Earl of. *Halifax: The Life of Lord Halifax*. Boston: Houghton Mifflin Company, 1965.

Blake, Robert, and William Roger Louis, eds. *Churchill: A Major New Assessment of His Life in Peace and War*. New York: W. W. Norton & Company, 1993.

Bonham-Carter, Lady Violet. *Winston Churchill: An Intimate Portrait*. New York: Harcourt, Brace & World, 1965.

Boswell, James. *The Life of Samuel Johnson*. London: Penguin Classics, 1986.

Botton, Alain de. *Kiss and Tell*. New York: Picador, 1995.

Brendon, Piers. *Winston Churchill: A Biography*. New York: Harper & Row, 1984.

Brittain, Vera. *Testament of Experience*. New York: Macmillan and Company, 1957.

Bullock, Alan. *Hitler: A Study in Tyranny*. New York: HarperPerennial, 1962.

Byatt, A. S. *The Biographer's Tale*. New York: Alfred A. Knopf, 2001.

Callahan, Raymond. *Churchill: Retreat from Empire*. Wilmington: Scholarly Resources, 1984.

Cannadine, David. *Aspects of Aristocracy*. New York: Penguin Books, 1994.

———. *History in Our Time*. New York: Penguin Books, 1998.

———. *Ornamentalism: How the British Saw Their Empire*. New York: Oxford University Press, 2001.

———, ed. *Blood, Toil, Tears, and Sweat: The Speeches of Winston Churchill*. Boston: Houghton Mifflin Company, 1989.

Charmley, John. *Churchill's Grand Alliance: The Anglo-American Special Relationship, 1940–57*. New York: Harvest Books, 1995.

———. *Churchill: The End of Glory*. New York: Harcourt, Brace and Company, 1993.

Churchill, Randolph. *Winston S. Churchill,* vols. 1–2. With companion volumes. Boston: Houghton Mifflin Company, 1966–1967.

Churchill, Sarah. *A Thread in the Tapestry*. London: André Deutsch, 1967.

Churchill, Winston. *Amid These Storms*. New York: Charles Scribner's Sons, 1932.

———. *Great Contemporaries*. Chicago: University of Chicago Press, 1937.

———. *A History of the English-Speaking Peoples*. 4 vols. New York: Dodd, Mead and Company, 1956–1958.

———. *Lord Randolph Churchill*. 2 vols. New York: Macmillan and Company, 1906.

———. *Marlborough: His Life and Times*. 6 vols. New York: Charles Scribner's Sons, 1933–1938.

———. *Maxims and Reflections*. Edited by Colin Coote. Boston: Houghton Mifflin Company, 1947.

———. *My African Journey*. New York: George H. Doran Company, 1908.

———. *My Early Life: A Roving Commission*. New York: Charles Scribner's Sons, 1930.

———. *Painting as a Pastime*. New York: Cornerstone, 1950.

———. *The River War*. London: Longmans, Green, and Company, 1899.

———. *Savrola*. New York: Random House, 1956.

———. *The Second World War*. 6 vols. Boston: Houghton Mifflin Company, 1948–1953.

———. *The World Crisis*. 5 vols. New York: Charles Scribner's Sons, 1923–1931.

Churchill, Winston S. *His Father's Son: The Life of Randolph Churchill*. London: Weidenfeld & Nicolson, 1996.

Clifford, James L., ed. *Biography as an Art: Selected Criticism, 1560–1960*. New York: Oxford University Press, 1962.

Cockshut, A.O.J. *Truth to Life: The Art of Biography in the Nineteenth Century*. New York: Harcourt Brace Jovanovich, 1974.

Colville, John. *The Fringes of Power: 10 Downing Street Diaries, 1939–1955*. New York: W. W. Norton & Company, 1985.

———. *Winston Churchill and His Inner Circle*. New York: Wyndham Books, 1981.

Coombs, David. *Churchill: His Paintings* (catalog). New York: World Publishing Company, 1967.

Cooper, Diana. *Trumpets from the Steep*. Boston: Houghton Mifflin Company, 1960.

Corrigan, Robert W., ed. *Tragedy: Vision and Form*. New York: Harper & Row, 1965.

Delafield, E. M. *The Provincial Lady in Wartime*. New York: Harper & Brothers, 1940.

Eade, Charles, ed. *Churchill by His Contemporaries*. London: Reprint Society, 1953.

Edel, Leon. *Literary Biography*. Toronto: University of Toronto Press, 1957.

———. *Writing Lives: Principia Biographica*. New York: W. W. Norton & Company, 1959.

Erikson, Erik. *Gandhi's Truth: On the Origins of Militant Nonviolence*. New York: W. W. Norton & Company, 1969.

Evans, Richard J. *In Defence of History*. London: Granta Books, 1997.

Feiling, Keith. *The Life of Neville Chamberlain*. Hamden: Archon Books, 1970.

Fleming, Kate. *The Churchills*. New York: Viking, 1975.

Fleming, Peter. *The Flying Visit*. New York: Charles Scribner's Sons, 1940.

———. *Operation Sea Lion: The Projected Invasion of England in 1940*. New York: Akadine Press, 1956.

Fuchs, Thomas. *A Concise Biography of Adolf Hitler*. New York: Berkley Books, 1990.

Fussell, Paul. *The Great War and Modern Memory*. New York: Oxford University Press, 1974.

———. *Wartime: Understanding and Behavior in the Second World War*. New York: Oxford University Press, 1989.

Gardner, Brian. *Churchill in Power: As Seen by His Contemporaries*. Boston: Houghton Mifflin Company, 1970.

Gathorne-Hardy, Jonathan. *The Unnatural History of the Nanny*. New York: Dial Press, 1973.

Gilbert, Martin. *Churchill: A Life*. New York: Henry Holt and Company, 1991.

————. *In Search of Churchill*. New York: John Wiley & Sons, 1994.

————. *Winston S. Churchill*, vols. 3–8. With companion volumes. Boston: Houghton Mifflin Company, 1971–1988.

Gittings, Robert. *The Nature of Biography*. Seattle: University of Washington Press, 1978.

Goebbels, Joseph. *Final Entries 1945: The Diaries of Joseph Goebbels*. Edited by Hugh Trevor-Roper. Translated by Richard Barry. New York: G. P. Putnam's Sons, 1978.

————. *The Goebbels Diaries, 1942–1943*. Edited and translated by Louis P. Lochner. New York: Doubleday and Company, 1948.

Golding, William. *The Paper Men*. New York: Farrar, Straus and Giroux, 1984.

Gorky, Maxim. *Reminiscences of Tolstoy, Chekhov and Andreev*. Translated by Katherine Mansfield, S. S. Koteliansky, and Leonard Woolf. London: Hogarth Press, 1968.

Graebner, Walter. *My Dear Mr. Churchill*. Boston: Riverside Press, 1965.

Graves, Robert. *Good-Bye to All That*. New York: Anchor Books, 1929.

Halifax, Earl of. *Fulness of Days*. New York: Dodd, Mead and Company, 1957.

Halle, Kay. *Irrepressible Churchill*. New York: World Publishing Company, 1966.

Hayward, Steven F. *Churchill on Leadership*. Rocklin: Prima, 1997.

Hitler, Adolf. *Hitler's Secret Conversations, 1941–1944*. Translated by N. Cameron and R. H. Stevens. Introduction by H. R. Trevor-Roper. New York: Farrar, Straus, & Young, 1953.

Hobsbawm, Eric, and Terence Ranger, eds. *The Invention of Tradition*. Cambridge: Cambridge University Press, 1983.

Holley, Darrell. *Churchill's Literary Allusions*. Jefferson: McFarland & Company, 1987.

Holmes, Richard. *Footsteps: Adventures of a Romantic Biographer*. New York: Penguin Books, 1985.

Homberger, Eric, and John Charmley, eds. *The Troubled Face of Biography*. New York: St. Martin's Press, 1988.

Hough, Richard. *Winston and Clementine*. New York: Bantam Books, 1990.

Howells, Roy. *Churchill's Last Years*. New York: David McKay Company, 1965.

Ismay, General Lord. *The Memoirs of General Lord Ismay*. New York: Viking Press, 1960.

James, Henry. *The Aspern Papers*. New York: Dell Publishing Company, 1959.

James, Lawrence. *Raj: The Making and Unmaking of British India*. New York: St. Martin's Press, 1997.

Jenkins, Roy. *Churchill*. New York: Farrar, Straus and Giroux, 2001.

Keegan, John. *The Face of Battle*. New York: Penguin Books, 1976.

———. *The Mask of Command*. New York: Penguin Books, 1987.

Kendall, Paul. *The Art of Biography*. London: Allen & Unwin, 1965.

Kennedy, David. *Freedom from Fear: The American People in Depression and War, 1929–1945*. New York: Oxford University Press, 1999.

Kershaw, Ian. *Hitler, 1936–1945: Nemesis*. New York: W. W. Norton & Company, 2000.

———. *The "Hitler Myth": Image and Reality in the Third Reich*. New York: Oxford University Press, 1987.

Kimball, Warren F. *Forged in War: Roosevelt, Churchill, and the Second World War*. New York: William Morrow & Company, 1997.

Kipling, Rudyard. *Plain Tales from the Hills*. New York: Penguin Books, 1987.

Koestenbaum, Wayne. *Jackie Under My Skin: Interpreting an Icon*. New York: Penguin Books, 1995.

Leslie, Anita. *Clare Sheridan*. Garden City: Doubleday and Company, 1977.

Lukacs, John. *Churchill: Visionary. Statesman. Historian*. New Haven: Yale University Press, 2002.

————. *The Duel: Hitler vs. Churchill: 10 May–31 July 1940*. London: Phoenix Press, 1990.

————. *Five Days in London: May 1940*. New Haven: Yale University Press, 1999.

————. *The Hitler of History*. New York: Vintage Books, 1997.

Lurie, Alison. *The Truth about Lorin Jones*. New York: Little, Brown and Company, 1988.

Malcolm, Janet. *The Crime of Sheila McGough*. New York: Vintage Books, 1999.

————. *The Silent Woman: Sylvia Plath and Ted Hughes*. New York: Vintage Books, 1993.

Manchester, William. *The Last Lion: Winston Spencer Churchill: Alone, 1932–1940*. Boston: Little, Brown and Company, 1988.

————. *The Last Lion: Winston Spencer Churchill: Visions of Glory, 1874–1932*. Boston: Little, Brown and Company, 1983.

Mandel, Oscar. *A Definition of Tragedy*. New York: New York University Press, 1961.

Masani, Zareer. *Indian Tales of the Raj*. Berkeley: University of California Press, 1987.

Maurois, André. *Aspects of Biography*. Translated by Sydney Castle Roberts. New York: D. Appleton and Company, 1929.

Mazower, Mark. *Dark Continent: Europe's Twentieth Century*. New York: Vintage Books, 1998.

Moir, Phyllis. *I Was Winston Churchill's Private Secretary*. New York: Wilfred Funk, Inc., 1941.

Moran, Lord. *Churchill: Taken from the Diaries of Lord Moran*. Boston: Houghton Mifflin Company, 1966.

Morris, James. *Farewell the Trumpets: An Imperial Retreat*. New York: Harcourt, Brace and Company, 1978.

————. *Pax Britannica: The Climax of an Empire*. New York: Harcourt, Brace and Company, 1968.

Morris, Jan. *Fisher's Face: Or, Getting to Know the Admiral*. New York: Random House, 1995.

Mosley, Leonard. *The Reich Marshal: A Biography of Hermann Goering*. New York: Doubleday and Company, 1974.

Murrow, Edward R. *This Is London*. Edited by Elmer Davis. New York: Schocken Books, 1941.

Nabokov, Vladimir. *Pale Fire*. New York: Vintage International, 1962.

Nadel, Ira Bruce. *Biography: Fiction, Fact, and Form*. New York: St. Martin's Press, 1984.

Nel, Elizabeth Layton. *Mr. Churchill's Secretary*. New York: Coward-McCann, 1958.

Nicolson, Sir Harold. *The Development of English Biography*. London: Hogarth Press, 1959.

———. *The English Sense of Humour and Other Essays*. New York: Funk & Wagnalls, 1968.

———. *Some People*. New York: Oxford University, Press, 1934.

———. *Diaries and Letters*, vol. 2, *The War Years, 1939–1945*. Edited by Nigel Nicolson. New York: Atheneum, 1967.

Novarr, David. *The Lines of Life: Theories of Biography, 1880–1970*. West Lafayette: Purdue University Press, 1986.

Pachter, Marc, ed. *Telling Lives: The Biographer's Art*. Washington, D.C.: New Republic Books, 1979.

Pagden, Anthony. *Peoples and Empires: A Short History of European Migration, Exploration, and Conquest, from Greece to the Present*. New York: Modern Library, 2001.

Parker, R.A.C. *Chamberlain and Appeasement: British Policy and the Coming of the Second World War*. London: Macmillan, 1993.

Pawle, Gerald. *The War and Colonel Warden*. New York: Alfred A. Knopf, 1963.

Paxman, Jeremy. *The English: A Portrait of a People*. New York: Overlook Press, 2000.

Pearson, John. *The Private Lives of Winston Churchill*. New York: Simon and Schuster, 1991.

Ponting, Clive. *Churchill*. London: Sinclair-Stevenson, 1994.

———. *1940: Myth and Reality*. Chicago: Ivan R. Dee, 1990.

Rhodes James, Robert. *Churchill: A Study in Failure, 1900–1939*. New York: World Publishing Company, 1970.

Roberts, Andrew. *Eminent Churchillians*. New York: Simon and Schuster, 1994.

————. *"The Holy Fox": The Life of Lord Halifax*. London: Phoenix Giant, 1991.

Rose, Norman. *Churchill: The Unruly Giant*. New York: Free Press, 1994.

Rose, Phyllis. *Parallel Lives: Five Victorian Marriages*. New York: Alfred A. Knopf, 1983.

Rosenbaum, Ron. *Explaining Hitler: The Search for the Origins of His Evil*. New York: HarperPerennial, 1998.

Sackville-West, Vita. *The Edwardians*. New York: Literary Guild of America, 1930.

Sassoon, Siegfried. *Siegfried's Journey, 1916–1920*. New York: Viking Press, 1946.

Scott, Paul. *The Day of the Scorpion*. Chicago: University of Chicago Press, 1968.

————. *A Division of the Spoils*. Chicago: University of Chicago Press, 1975.

————. *The Jewel in the Crown*. Chicago: University of Chicago Press, 1966.

————. *The Towers of Silence*. Chicago: University of Chicago Press, 1971.

Skidelsky, Robert. *John Maynard Keynes*, vol. 3, *Fighting for Freedom, 1937–1946*. New York: Viking, 2000.

Snow, C. P. *Variety of Men*. New York: Charles Scribner's Sons, 1966.

Soames, Mary. *Clementine Churchill: The Biography of a Marriage*. Boston: Houghton Mifflin Company, 1979.

————. *Family Album*. Boston: Houghton Mifflin Company, 1982.

————, ed. *Winston and Clementine: The Personal Letters of the Churchills*. New York: Houghton Mifflin Company, 1999.

Sontag, Susan. *On Photography*. New York: Anchor Books, 1977.

Speer, Albert. *Inside the Third Reich*. Translated by Richard and Clara Winston. New York: Touchstone, 1970.

Stafford, David. *Roosevelt and Churchill: Men of Secrets*. New York: Overlook Press, 1999.

Stevenson, Frances. *Lloyd George: A Diary*. New York: Harper & Row, 1971.

Storr, Anthony. *Churchill's Black Dog, Kafka's Mice, and Other Phenomena of the Human Mind*. London: William Collins Sons and Company, 1965.

Strachey, Lytton. *Biographical Essays*. New York: Harcourt, Brace and Company, 1949.

————. *Elizabeth and Essex*. London: Chatto and Windus, 1928.

————. *Eminent Victorians*. New York: Harcourt Brace Jovanovich, 1918.

————. *Literary Essays*. New York: Harcourt, Brace and Company, 1949.

————. *Queen Victoria*. New York: Harcourt, Brace and Company, 1921.

Strawson, John. *Churchill and Hitler: In Victory and Defeat*. New York: Fromm International, 1997.

Symons, A.J.A. *The Quest for Corvo: An Experiment in Biography*. Hopewell: Ecco Press, 1955.

Szarkowski, John. *The Photographer's Eye*. New York: Museum of Modern Art, 1966.

Taylor, A.J.P. *English History, 1914–1945*. Oxford History of England. Oxford: Oxford University Press, 1965.

————. *Englishmen and Others*. London: Hamish Hamilton, 1956.

————. *The Origins of the Second World War*. New York: Atheneum, 1961.

————. *A Personal History*. New York: Atheneum, 1983.

————. *The Warlords*. New York: Atheneum, 1978.

Taylor, A.J.P., Robert Rhodes James, J. H. Plumb, Basil Liddell Hart, and Anthony Storr. *Churchill Revised: A Critical Assessment*. New York: Dial Press, 1969.

Trevor-Roper, H. R. *The Last Days of Hitler*. New York: Macmillan and Company, 1947.

Waugh, Evelyn. *Put Out More Flags*. Boston: Little, Brown and Company, 1942.

Wheeler-Bennett, Sir John, ed. *Action This Day: Working with Churchill*. New York: St. Martin's Press, 1969.

Woolf, Leonard. *Downhill All the Way: An Autobiography of the Years 1919 to 1939*. New York: Harcourt Brace Jovanovich, 1967.

————. *The Journey Not the Arrival Matters: An Autobiography of the Years 1939 to 1969*. New York: Harcourt, Brace & World, 1969.

Woolf, Virginia. *Collected Essays*. Vol. 4. New York: Harcourt, Brace & World, 1953.

————. *Flush: A Biography*. New York: Harcourt, Brace and Company, 1933.

————. *Jacob's Room*. London: Hogarth Press, 1922.

————. *Orlando: A Biography*. New York: Harcourt Brace Jovanovich, 1928.

————. *Roger Fry: A Biography*. London: Hogarth Press, 1940.

ACKNOWLEDGMENTS

My deep thanks go to the two people who made *Forty Ways to Look at Winston Churchill* possible, my agent, Christy Fletcher, and my editor, Nancy Miller.

Special thanks to those who commented on *Forty Ways* at its various stages: Elizabeth Bogner, David Brock, Matthew Doull, Julie Hilden, Jed Weissberg, and particularly Reed Hundt, and my parents, Karen and Jack Craft. Stuart Vance did a wonderful job designing my Web site.

Last, thanks to Jamie, my long-suffering, revision-reading, morale-boosting husband, and to my sister Elizabeth, my best reader and friend.

INDEX

Note: Winston Churchill is referred to as W. C.

Permission Acknowledgments

Text

The author gratefully acknowledges the permission granted by the Masters, Fellows and Scholars of Churchill College, Cambridge, for the use of an excerpt from the letter of Clementine Churchill to Winston Churchill dated June 27, 1940.

Quotations from *My Early Life: A Roving Commission* by Winston Churchill, pages 2, 3, 18, 23, 84, 93, 94, 105, 106, 153, 180, 181, 210, and 223 reprinted with the permission of Scribner, an imprint of Simon & Schuster Adult Publishing Group and Curtis Brown Ltd., London, from *My Early Life: A Roving Commission* by Winston Churchill. Copyright © 1930 by Charles Scribner's Sons; Copyright renewed © 1958 by Winston Churchill.

Quotations from *Painting as a Pastime* and *The Second World War: Their Finest Hour* by Winston Churchill, from *Winston and Clementine: The Personal Letters of the Churchills* edited by Mary Soames, Copyright © Lady Soames, and from *Winston S. Churchill* by Randolph Churchill and Martin Gilbert, reproduced with permission of Curtis Brown Ltd., London, on behalf of Winston S. Churchill. Copyright © Winston S. Churchill.

Quotations from *The Oaken Heart* by Margery Allingham reproduced with permission of Curtis Brown Group Ltd., London, on behalf of Rights Ltd. Copyright © Margery Allingham 1941.

Photographs

Page

12   *Winston Churchill, June 1943.*
     Photo © Hulton–Deutsch Collection/CORBIS

21   *Winston Churchill, August 1944.*
     Photo © CORBIS

70   *The uniform, the cigar, and the V sign . . .*
     Photo © Bettman/CORBIS

91   *In May 1944, touring with Dominion Prime Ministers . . .*
     Photo © Bettman/CORBIS

108   *Lord Randolph Churchill, a few years before his death.*
     Photo © Bettman/CORBIS

114   *Churchill painted only one picture during World War II . . .*
     Photo © Bettman/CORBIS

154   *Winston and Clementine, a week before their marriage . . .*
     Photo © Bettman/CORBIS

155   *Clementine kisses Winston on his return to London . . .*
     Photo courtesy of AP/Wide World Photos

162   *A two-year-old Winston leans against his mother . . .*
     Photo courtesy of AP/Wide World Photos

162   *With his sailor suit, Churchill, aged seven . . .*
     Photo © Bettman/CORBIS

163   *1895. Churchill, a subaltern, in the ornate full-dress uniform . . .*
     Photo © Hulton–Deutsch Collection/CORBIS

163   *Churchill, a flying enthusiast, stands beside . . .*
     Photo © Hulton–Deutsch Collection/CORBIS

164   *In July 1925, Churchill is dressed for a polo match . . .*
     Photo © Hulton–Deutsch Collection/CORBIS

164   *1939. Churchill confers with the main proponent . . .*
     Photo © Hulton–Deutsch Collection/CORBIS

165   *September 1940. Winston and Clementine inspect . . .*
     Photo courtesy of AP/Wide World Photos

165   *November 1964. On the eve of his ninetieth birthday . . .*
     Photo © Hulton–Deutsch Collection/CORBIS

166   *September 1940. Churchill—an instantly recognizable silhouette . . .*
      Photo © Bettman/CORBIS
166   *August 1941. Roosevelt and Churchill lead hymn singing . . .*
      Photo courtesy of AP/Wide World Photos
167   *August 1941. Back in England, Churchill acknowledges . . .*
      Photo courtesy of AP/Wide World Photos
167   *Soon after returning from his meeting with President Roosevelt . . .*
      Photo courtesy of AP/Wide World Photos
168   *February 1945. The "Big Three" at Yalta . . .*
      Photo courtesy of AP/Wide World Photos
168   *On the evening of victory, May 8, 1945 . . .*
      Photo © Bettman/CORBIS
169   *In Berlin, July 1945, amid the wreck of Hitler's chancellery . . .*
      Photo © Hulton–Deutsch Collection/CORBIS
169   *January 1950. A seventy-five-year-old Churchill paints . . .*
      Photo © Bettman/CORBIS
170   *April 1955. Churchill holds the door . . .*
      Photo © Hulton–Deutsch Collection/CORBIS
170   *1965. After a service . . .*
      Photo courtesy of AP/Wide World Photos
204   *Blenheim Palace was the nation's gift to John Churchill . . .*
      Photo courtesy of AP/Wide World Photos
220   *Hitler gives the Nazi salute.*
      Photo © Bettman/CORBIS
220   *Churchill flashes the V sign.*
      Photo © Bettman/CORBIS
245   *Churchill, portrayed by Graham Sutherland.*
      Photo courtesy of AP/Wide World Photos
245   *Churchill and his portrait, photographed during the eightieth-birthday celebration.*
      Photo courtesy of AP/Wide World Photos
255   *Statue of Winston Churchill in the snow.*
      Photo © Bettman/CORBIS